EYES ON THE ENEMY

U.S. Military Intelligence in World War II

CHRIS MCNAB

CASEMATE

Philadelphia & Oxford

Published in the United States of America and Great Britain in 2023 by
CASEMATE PUBLISHERS
1950 Lawrence Road, Havertown, PA 19083, USA
and
The Old Music Hall, 106–108 Cowley Road, Oxford OX4 1JE, UK

Copyright © 2023 Casemate Publishers

Hardback Edition: ISBN 978-1-63624-384-9
Digital Edition: ISBN 978-1-63624-385-6

A CIP record for this book is available from the British Library

Printed and bound in the United Kingdom by CPI Group (UK) Ltd, Croydon, CR0 4YY
Typeset in India by DiTech Publishing Services

For a complete list of Casemate titles, please contact:

CASEMATE PUBLISHERS (US)
Telephone (610) 853-9131
Fax (610) 853-9146
Email: casemate@casematepublishers.com
www.casematepublishers.com

CASEMATE PUBLISHERS (UK)
Telephone (0)1226 734350
Email: casemate-uk@casematepublishers.co.uk
www.casematepublishers.co.uk

Cover image: MGen E. R. Quaseda, conducting a briefing for LtGen Carl Spaatz and LtGen James
Doolittle, VII Corps Headquarters, Münsterbusch, Germany, 1944. (U.S. Army Signal Corps)

Contents

Introduction

Intelligence is a crucial element of warfare, albeit one not always fully understood nor practiced coherently. Having prior eyes and ears on the enemy, either through covert observation, spies, prisoner interrogations, intercepted communications, or any other means, can bring key operational advantages, potentially ones significant enough to bring victory in either an individual battle or an entire war. Information collection is but a single part of the equation; also required is capable analysis and interpretation. Raw data and information are, on their own, a frequently confusing and contradictory mass, replete with blind alleys, red herrings, and irrelevant or outdated facts. What is needed is trained personnel to sift through and make sense of the inputs, bringing out the logical patterns and conclusions that lead to coherent decisions. Good intelligence handling also needs polished coordination, to rationalize and distribute the intelligence to those who need it without alerting the enemy to your special insight.

Historically, the military intelligence community has also often wrestled under something of an image problem. It frequently attracts suspicion and opprobrium in equal measures, either for its furtive or hidden activities, which can make it appear somewhat unaccountable or even inactive, or because of its failings—to frontline troops, intelligence can be more visible by its failures than its successes. Never was this more apparent than on December 7, 1941.

On that day, the U.S. Pacific Fleet Base at Pearl Harbor, Hawaii, was ripped apart under the bombs and torpedoes of Japanese carrier aircraft, the onslaught plunging the United States into a now-expanded World War II. To a degree, the United States had been preparing for war since the late 1930s, but the unforeseen shock of the Pearl Harbor attack left the nation reeling. Its military intelligence community, meanwhile, was humiliated. Evidently, Japan had slipped a prodigious operation against U.S. territory through achingly wide holes in the intelligence net. At the time, the main U.S. intelligence source on Japan was MAGIC, the code name given to encrypted high-level Japanese signals traffic, the most important of which was the PURPLE diplomatic code. The code had been broken by U.S. cryptanalysts in 1940, but Pearl Harbor demonstrated that PURPLE was largely irrelevant for military operation al insight. The more relevant code of the Japanese Navy, JN-25, was still resisting the efforts of codebreakers; furthermore, the Japanese Striking Force—composed of more than 50 combat vessels and 350 aircraft—kept fastidious radio silence until the attack was launched. Given that just four days later Germany also declared war on the United States, it was clear that U.S. military intelligence was in dire need of reform.

The main intelligence instruments of the U.S. military in the immediate aftermath of World War I (1914–18) were the U.S. Army's Military Intelligence Division (MID) and the U.S. Navy's venerable Office of Naval Intelligence (ONI), the latter founded in 1882 while the former had its roots in the recent world war. Like many branches of the U.S. armed forces, the MID suffered heavily from post-war demilitarization, the effects of which stretched deep into the inter-war years—by 1934 it had only 20 officers and 50 civilian support staff. On top of its actual intelligence-gathering activities, it also had to double-up Army public relations duties, a clear indication that intelligence at this time was taken less than seriously. The principal sources of intelligence were either U.S. foreign attachés or businesspeople recruited to make observations on trips abroad; typically, neither of these sources yielded high-grade military insight.

As the 1930s progressed, technological innovations provided the MID with new routes of intelligence gathering, including radar, radio interception, and aerial reconnaissance and photography (the aerial component in collaboration with the Army Air Corps). But the biggest advance in U.S. intelligence during the pre-war years came in the field of cryptology (the practice of designing secure communications) and signal intelligence (SIGINT), technology-driven fields that stood in contrast to human intelligence (HUMINT). Responsibility for SIGINT and cryptology was split between several organizations during the 1920s, but in 1930 it was integrated into the Signal Intelligence Service (SIS), part of the Signal Corps, and headed by cryptographer William Frederick Friedman. By this time the Navy had already established its own SIGINT unit, the Communication Security Unit, or OP-20-G. (Later, in World War II, the SIS evolved into the Signal Security Service and then, from 1943, the Signal Security Agency.)

By 1939, the United States was aware that the war clouds gathering over Europe might eventually drift its way, thus efforts were made to give the intelligence infrastructure more scale and scope. MID was expanded and a Counterintelligence Branch was established in 1939, focused on countering foreign espionage in the domestic armed forces. An agency with a similar remit was the Army's Corps of Intelligence Police (CIP), an internal investigative body founded in World War I and succeeded by the Counter Intelligence Corps (CIC) in 1942. Domestically, however, the main body tasked with counterintelligence was the Federal Bureau of Investigation (FBI).

The actual outbreak of war in Europe in September 1939 galvanized the further expansion of U.S. military intelligence across the board in 1940–41. The MID swelled moderately to a force of 200 officers and 848 civilians, while the U.S. Army Air Corps (USAAC) received its own organic intelligence units, as did the Corps of Engineers, which had a special responsibility for handling cartographic intelligence (intelligence derived from maps or charts). SIS also expanded on the back of its breaking of the Japanese PURPLE communications, and its parent formation, the Signal Corps, took responsibility for the development of radar-collected intelligence and radar security. Crucially, the early war years also saw the beginnings of strengthening transatlantic intelligence cooperation between Britain and the United States, which would become fruitful in the field of SIGINT and code-breaking.

Another notable event was the foundation, in June 1941, of a new espionage service, led by highly capable lawyer and much-decorated World War I hero William J. Donovan. Despite hostility towards Donovan's enterprise from the MID, who naturally saw it as treading on their turf (they set up their own "Psychological Warfare" section in response), and the poor quality of much early intelligence gleaned, Donovan's efforts would lead to the establishment of the Office of Strategic Services (OSS) in 1942. The OSS, an agency of the Joint Chiefs of Staff (JCS), grew to have 13,000 personnel and would take central responsibility for the development and coordination of espionage behind enemy lines in the European, East Asian, and African theaters.

As the United States moved from the sidelines of a world war to being an active combatant, it became critical to enforce better interservice intelligence liaison and pool intelligence in the most effective way. Thus, a Joint Intelligence Committee (JIC) was established on December 11, 1941, (although planning for this had actually begun before the Pearl Harbor attack), bringing together the heads of the MID and ONI and resulting in a certain degree of Army/Navy cooperation, including the production of joint intelligence studies. Greater changes came in the spring of 1942, when the Army divided itself into Army Ground Forces, Army Air Forces, and Services of Supply, each of which now had its own intelligence staff and structure. These changes meant that the MID was drastically reduced in size and scope, with its intelligence-gathering role passing to a new organization, the Military Intelligence Service (MIS), which had a complement of 342 officers and 1,000 other personnel by April 1942. The MIS included, from May 1942, a Special Branch sub-section which handled the processing and distribution of communications intelligence, in an effort to break down some of the intelligence silos that prevented the flow of information to those who needed it. The Special Branch would play an important role in handling both MAGIC and ULTRA. The latter was the British military intelligence code name for signals intelligence obtained by breaking high-level encrypted German radio and teleprinter communications, the British work conducted at the Government Code and Cypher School (GC&CS) at Bletchley Park in Buckinghamshire, England. The distribution of such information required a deft touch to avoid alerting the enemy to the fact that the Allies had access, albeit variable, to its more secure communications traffic. Indeed, the growth in handling ULTRA was one factor behind a further major redesign in the U.S. intelligence architecture in 1944. Special Branch was reformed to handle ULTRA specifically, and MIS was separated from MID and divided into three directorates: Administration, Intelligence, and Information. Later, MIS would also take operational control over the Signal Security Agency.

SIGINT in particular grew to be a huge U.S. enterprise in World War II, with a total of 26,000 personnel working in the field on everything from intercepting enemy radio traffic to enforcing security measures over U.S. transmissions. The strategic significance, intellectual effort, and technological advances made in the field of high-level Allied SIGINT, however, have tended to obscure the fact that much U.S. intelligence activity was conducted at far lower levels, through the dangerous yet more workaday activities of frontline combat intelligence staff. The U.S. Army, for example, had intelligence units embedded from theater HQs down to battalion level, the intelligence staffs collecting and processing endless information inputs from HUMINT, SIGINT, and other sources. Inputs came from a range of sources: from captured documents to interrogated POWs; aerial photographs to combat troops observation reports; and tactical signals intelligence through to censored letters. It was an effort that demanded great investment in recruitment and training infrastructure, and special breeds of individuals with highly perceptive and analytical minds. Foreign-language skills and a knowledge of enemy cultures and military systems were at a premium. Tens of thousands of soldiers and civilians were put through intelligence training across the continental United States to feed the system. The MIS, for example, trained more than 4,800 Japanese language translators alone to work in the Pacific theater, many of these individuals being second-generation Japanese Americans, known as Nisei.

Frontline SIGINT was also crucial to the efficacy of combat intelligence, and both the technologies and procedures were refined during the war. Mobile tactical signals units accompanied most major frontline units and formations, assisting in communications security while also conducting real-time monitoring of enemy radio traffic. The things that were said by the enemy on the radio were not the only elements of value to the U.S. radio operators, indeed, often the actual words made the least important contribution. Instead, the signalers would derive important intelligence clues from seemingly secondary aspects, such as the mere volume of traffic, the strength of the signals, or the direction from which the communications came.

In additional to combat SIGINT, other types of frontline intelligence teams included interrogators (specializing in the interrogation of enemy POWs and of civilians who had been behind enemy lines), photographic interpreters, and order of battle analysts. There were also engineer intelligence units that oversaw the production of topographic intelligence, derived from aerial photography. All these intelligence activities would be brought together under the guidance of G-2 intelligence staff at divisional level and above, or S-2 staff at battalion or brigade levels.

There were some significant differences between the European Theater of Operations (ETO) and Mediterranean Theater of Operations (MTO) on the one hand, and the Pacific Theater of Operations (PTO) on the other. In the latter, much of the intelligence work rested in the hands of the Navy and the Marine Corps; the latter established an M-2 intelligence staff in 1939. The South West Pacific Area (SWPA), which rested under the imperious command of General Douglas MacArthur, made some unilateral innovations. MacArthur directed the development of the SWPA's own cryptologic branch based in Australia—the Central Bureau, Brisbane. It also formed a new type of Special Forces unit, the all-volunteer ALAMO Scouts (U.S. 6th Army Special Reconnaissance Unit), to conduct long-range intelligence-gathering operations. Commanded by Lieutenant General Walter Krueger, Commanding General of the U.S. Sixth Army, and having undergone some of the toughest military training of any Allied unit during the war, the ALAMO Scouts had the exceptional war record of more than one hundred operations undertaken behind enemy lines without the loss of a single man. It should be noted, however, that MacArthur had no time for the OSS, a unit that he barred from operating in the SWPA.

By the end of the war, the U.S. intelligence domain was a large and sprawling entity. It was not beyond criticism. It contained within its disparate structure a great many inefficiencies, duplications, and operational gaps. But collectively, and alongside the efforts of other Allied intelligence organizations, the U.S. military intelligence community gave American forces on the ground at least a partial window into the tactical and strategic thinking going on across enemy lines. Thus, critical failures, such as the wide-eyed surprise of Germany's Ardennes offensive in late 1944, were balanced by major successes, especially in the Pacific—the ONI's discovery of Japanese battleplans around Midway in June 1942 helped change the direction of the Pacific War in favor of the U.S.

In this volume, we have collected a broad range of official manuals and documents from the U.S. intelligence community during World War II. Given the degree to which the ULTRA and PURPLE stories are told elsewhere, our main focus here is on combat intelligence, the skills, procedures, technologies, and tactics needed to discover enemy intentions on the frontlines. We also devote chapters to the activities of OSS and counterintelligence operatives, to combat SIGINT, aerial reconnaissance, and core naval intelligence procedures. What is often implicit in these documents is that intelligence gathering was not just a matter of sitting safely behind the lines monitoring radio traffic or opening captured mail. Many intelligence operators went deep into the heart of the combat, experiencing warfighting up close even as they tried to make rational sense of the often terrible things they were seeing and hearing.

CHAPTER I

Organization, Objectives, and Training

As the main introduction to this book explained, the intelligence infrastructure of the United States during World War II was multi-layered, and not always coherently so. But whatever the nature of the individual intelligence organizations and units—from high-level government cryptanalysis conducted stateside down to company-sized Army intelligence units in the combat theaters—all efforts were ultimately guided by the core principles of military intelligence. The overarching definition was laid down in the following manual, Military Intelligence: Combat Intelligence (FM 30-5, 1940): "Military intelligence is evaluated and interpreted information concerning a possible or actual enemy, or theater of operations, together with the conclusions drawn therefrom. It includes information concerning enemy capabilities or possible lines of action open to him, as well as all that relates to the territory controlled by him or subject to his influence."

U.S. military intelligence was further subdivided into two practical categories: combat intelligence and War Department intelligence. The former related to frontline intelligence efforts conducted under actual conditions of war against an active enemy. Typically, the focus of combat intelligence was anything that could give American forces an advantageous tactical insight into the enemy's intentions and operations, or external factors that might affect the same. Examples of the foci of combat intelligence therefore include: dispositions, terrain, tactics, armaments, supply situation, morale, combat losses, vehicles, and equipment. Much of this sort of intelligence was gathered by direct observation, aerial reconnaissance, prisoner interrogation, and document analysis. At the higher level was War Department intelligence, which focused on the broadest strategic picture, not only analyzing *the armed forces of enemies both potential and real, but also political, economic, social, ideological, geographical, and many other contexts packaging the threat.*

In this chapter, we focus on combat intelligence, drawing on the Combat Intelligence *manual in particular. It usefully summarizes the organization, objectives, procedures, and training of combat intelligence personnel. Regarding the latter, the greatest of the training establishments was the Military Intelligence Training Center (MITC) at Camp Ritchie, Maryland, which handled the instruction of more than 19,000 intelligence personnel during the war years. Given the intellectual range of the syllabi explained in the text below, it is evident that those who emerged from Camp Ritchie or other intelligence training programs were generally individuals of above-average capabilities.*

★★★

From FM 30-5, *Basic Field Manual, Military Intelligence: Combat Intelligence* (1940)

SECTION I
GENERAL

[. . .]

■ 4. MILITARY INTELLIGENCE IN COMMANDER'S DECISION.—*a.* The commander's decision is based upon the mission as affected by the following:

(1) Enemy to be dealt with in accomplishing the mission.

(2) Terrain over which the operation must be conducted.

(3) Means available for the execution of the mission.

b. Before making a decision initiating action designed to accomplish his mission, the commander will need information concerning the two unknown factors, enemy and terrain; having made a decision, he will require information which will permit him to continue projected operations and accomplish his mission regardless of what the enemy may do, or to make a new decision in view of the changed situation. Military intelligence thus plays a direct part in every decision, the soundness of which will depend in each case upon the accuracy of information regarding the two unknown factors and upon the ability of the commander to understand correctly the influence of the various factors upon the problem. Consequently, for each decision of the commander there should be, whenever appropriate, an intelligence plan designed to coordinate the search for definite information which the particular situation demands.

■ 5. OBJECT OF COMBAT INTELLIGENCE.—*a.* The primary object of combat intelligence work is to reduce as far as possible uncertainties regarding the enemy and local conditions and thus assist the commander in making a decision and the troops in executing their assigned missions.

b. The secondary object of combat intelligence work is to assist the commander in the formulation and supervision of counterintelligence measures designed to conceal our own intentions and activities and to defeat measures adopted by the enemy for the purpose of influencing our own actions.

■ 6. DIFFICULTIES INVOLVED IN OBTAINING ADEQUATE INFORMATION.— The difficulties involved in obtaining adequate information and in arriving at reliable conclusions based thereon are many. These difficulties are due principally to the fact that the interests of the enemy demand that he shall make every possible effort to foil our attempts to gain information. He will conceal his movements by night marches and counterintelligence measures involving the use of both ground and air agencies; he will make use of ground and cover to conceal his movements and will supplement natural cover with camouflage; he will resort to any tactical measures that offer a reasonable chance of obtaining secrecy or surprise; he will enforce a strict censorship and enforce cryptographic security measures to prevent leaks of information; he may distribute false information and institute measures to deceive our collecting agencies; and he will sometimes adopt a course of action that may appear illogical. The opposition of the enemy's interest to our own, as well as the independence of his will, must necessarily make him more or less an unknown factor in every situation. To a lesser degree, the terrain also is an unknown factor.

SECTION II
INTELLIGENCE FUNCTIONS AND ORGANIZATION

■ 7. UNIT COMMANDER.—Since intelligence constitutes a vital element in the commander's estimate of the situation leading to a decision, it is a basic function of command to initiate and coordinate the search for the necessary information. In addition, a commander may receive reconnaissance missions or demands for specific information from higher authority as well as requests for information from lower and neighboring units. These may or may not coincide with his own requirements for information. In any case, each commander is responsible for obtaining all military information which is essential to his own unit, whether by his own means or by requests on higher or neighboring headquarters. Conversely, within his own zone of operations he is responsible for collecting such information as is requested by higher headquarters, and so far as practicable, such as is requested by lower and neighboring units. By this system a commander, with due regard to the mobility of any forces that the enemy may possibly possess, particularly mechanized and motorized, is enabled to extend his search for information in sufficient depth and width to guard against surprise.

■ 8. ASSISTANT CHIEF OF STAFF, G-2.—*Wherever the term "assistant chief of staff, G-2" or "G-2" is used in this manual it is interpreted to include the intelligence officer or S-2 of all lower units.*

a. At the headquarters of every combat unit, the G-2 will keep the commander and all interested staff officers informed regarding the enemy situation and of his deductions concerning it.

b. Under the supervision and direction of the chief of staff or the unit commander, it will be the duty of G-2 to—

(1) Specify the information to be gathered.

(2) Initiate a systematic and coordinated search for required information by all available collecting agencies.

(3) Collate, evaluate, and interpret information derived from all possible sources.

(4) Reduce intelligence to a systematic form and distribute it to all concerned in time to be of value to the recipients.

(5) Insure that intelligence is given due consideration in the preparation of plans, and that orders, formal or fragmentary, are checked to see that this has been done.

(6) Insure that counterintelligence measures are given due consideration in the preparation of plans, and that orders, formal or fragmentary, are checked to see that this has been done

(7) Supervise mapping activities and assure an adequate supply and distribution of maps and map substitutes.

(8) Coordinate requests for aerial photographs and in some echelons determine their distribution.

(9) Maintain close liaison with the G-2 section of higher, lower, and adjacent units.

(10) Exercise general supervision over all intelligence activities and, whenever directed by the commanding officer, intelligence training in the unit.

■ 9. DUAL FUNCTIONS.—The military intelligence section is one of the coordinate sections of every general staff and of similarly organized staffs. It has operative functions as well as general staff functions which vary in scope with the size of the command. In the lower units, the operative functions may be confined to observation and the examination of prisoners and documents, while at GHQ they include publicity, counterpropaganda, censorship, control of visitors, counterespionage, espionage, and others.

■ 10. PRINCIPLES OF ORGANIZATION.—*a.* The intelligence section should be able to handle information of a scope commensurate with the size and mission of the command. It should be so organized and equipped that it will fit into the living and working conditions of the command in all situations while retaining the degree of mobility essential to the arm; and its organization should facilitate the collection, collation, evaluation, and interpretation of information as well as prompt dissemination of the resulting intelligence to all concerned.

b. In the division and lower combat units, the primary functions of the intelligence section are the collection, collation, evaluation, and interpretation of information, and dissemination of combat intelligence.

The organization should be simple; methods employed should insure speed; and facilities available at headquarters should be appropriate to the unit and the arm concerned. Complete details of operation are contained in the Field Manuals for the respective arms.

Section III
COLLECTION OF INFORMATION

■ 11. COORDINATION.—Ability of the enemy to act in various ways within his assigned mission and the limited and diverse nature of information gathering agencies available to the commander require an understanding of enemy capabilities and the most careful coordination of all intelligence activities.

a. Enemy capabilities.—(1) In any situation, the lines of action of which the enemy is physically capable and which can possibly affect the accomplishment or manner of execution of our mission are called the enemy capabilities for that particular situation. The term "capabilities" includes not only the general lines of action open to the enemy, such as attack, defense, or withdrawal, but also all the particular lines of action possible under each general line of action. For example, under the general line of action of an attack, the various particular lines of action possible are an attack today, an attack tomorrow, an envelopment of our left flank, an uncoordinated attack against our front, and others.

(2) In order that the commander may arrive at a new decision or decide to adhere to an old one, he must, from time to time, make an estimate of the situation. As an essential part of such an estimate, he must obtain, ordinarily from G-2, factual data as to the combat strength of the enemy confronting him and as to the possible strength and time of arrival of reinforcements. In addition, the commander with the assistance of G-2 must arrive at conclusions relative to the enemy's capabilities and the effect of time, space, terrain, and other conditions upon each of these.

(3) The commander's initial decision, however, must be supplemented by other decisions as the action progresses. These decisions must be based on a narrowing down of the enemy capabilities previously considered. Accordingly, intelligence activities should be so directed as to investigate

each capability with a view to finally determining which of his capabilities the enemy is actually adopting. This can be accomplished only by obtaining information which gradually eliminates certain capabilities and eventually enables G-2 to determine the line of action the enemy has adopted. If this process is based upon faulty interpretation or upon inadequate or inaccurate information, there is always danger that the enemy may gain surprise.

b. Essential elements of information.—(1) The essential elements of information consist of that information of the enemy, of the terrain not under our control, or of meteorological conditions in territory held by the enemy which a commander needs to make a sound decision, conduct a maneuver, avoid surprise, or formulate details of a plan of operations. The essential elements are designated for the purpose of focusing the attention and activities of all collecting agencies on that information which, from the viewpoint of the commander, is necessary at a particular time. They include questions relating to enemy capabilities, other intelligence specifically desired by the commander, and information requested by other units.

(2) It is the duty of the commander to obtain correct information bearing upon his mission and to insure coordination of all collecting agencies at his disposal. He is therefore responsible for the designation of essential elements of information. He makes basic decisions and exercises the continuing supervision which insure that the intelligence effort is directed along proper lines. In determining essential elements, however, he is assisted by his chief of staff and G-2. G-2 should study continuously in collaboration with other members of the staff, particularly G-3, our own and the enemy situation, possible lines of action open to the enemy, and the influence of terrain and other local conditions on these lines of action. Based on this study, G-2 should at all times be prepared to recommend to the commander the essential elements of information and to give the important considerations governing their selection.

NOTE.—Wherever the term "G-3" is used in this manual it is interpreted to include the S-3 of all lower combat units.

(3) As a standing procedure and without a special directive the following will be considered as essential elements in appropriate situations:

(*a*) In an advance by the enemy, the number, strength composition, and direction of movement of columns and probable place of contact.

(*b*) In an attack by the enemy, the direction and weight of the main effort.

(*c*) In a defense by the enemy, the flanks, and strength, composition, and location of reserves capable of intervening.

(*d*) In an enemy retrograde movement, the direction of movement and location of demolitions and defensive positions.

(*e*) In a pursuit by the enemy, the strength, composition, location, and direction of movement of encircling forces and where they will make contact.

(*f*) In projected operations, the nature, location, and condition of natural and man–made obstacles to our maneuver and the determination of important terrain features not shown on available maps.

(4) For purposes of orientation, either the commander in his directive or G–2 should acquaint the staff with the essential elements and with any modifications of them. If an intelligence annex is issued, the essential elements are stated therein. If no annex is issued, they are communicated to subordinate commanders if practicable.

(5) Essential elements may be expressed in the form of a question or in the form of a statement as to information desired. If expressed as a question, it should be understood that no guess as to enemy intentions is desired, but that search is to be directed for facts which will disclose, progressively, the confirmation or elimination of the capability to which the inquiry relates.

■ 12. INFORMATION NOT LIMITED TO ESSENTIAL ELEMENTS.—The essential elements of information are guides governing the search for information and not limitations regulating the information to be reported. Therefore, collecting agencies will transmit all enemy information which comes to their attention.

■ 13. NATURE OF INFORMATION REQUIRED.—In order to determine the type of information required to answer the essential elements of information, G-2 must understand the object and scope of the study and the sources and significance of information. The following are some of the considerations he should take into account:

a. Study of terrain.—(1) *Sources of information.*—The sources of information for a study of the terrain are maps; vertical and oblique aerial photographs; personal reconnaissance, when possible; troops, particularly Cavalry and Air Corps; inhabitants and agents; enemy documents; and geographical reports from higher headquarters.

(2) *Responsibility.*—G-2 is responsible for the study of the terrain from the point of view of the enemy, and the collection of information as to the terrain and meteorological conditions in territory held by the enemy.

(3) *Estimate of terrain held by us from viewpoint of enemy.*—(*a*) Based upon his knowledge of the enemy situation and of the enemy's probable knowledge of our own situation, G-2 should determine the favorable and unfavorable effects of the terrain on all possible lines of action which may be adopted by the enemy.

(*b*) For operations of the corps and lower units, the estimate is prepared after a detailed study of relief, natural and artificial obstacles, communication, and cover. If time permits, preparation of the estimate may be facilitated by special maps upon which stream lines and ridge lines have been plainly marked.

(*c*) In the higher echelons of command, G-2 should give careful consideration to the influence of economic resources, natural and artificial obstacles, and communication of territory under our control upon possible plans open to the enemy.

(4) *Terrain not under our control.*—(*a*) A study of terrain not under our control should include such matters as are directly necessitated by the essential elements of information, if any, relating to the terrain. In addition, G-2 should ascertain from G-3 whether any features should be investigated with respect to their effect on details of our contemplated maneuver. This is particularly important with respect to obstacles to our maneuver whose present condition is not disclosed by available maps.

(*b*) In the higher echelons of command, economic resources, natural and artificial obstacles, and communication within the enemy's territory will be subjects of special studies by G-2.

(5) *Meteorological conditions.*—Although meteorological conditions do not constitute a part of a terrain study, nevertheless they have such an immediate and important relation to terrain that they should be included in the study.

b. *Study of the enemy.*—(1) *Importance.*—The enemy represents the most uncertain factor. No matter how painstakingly information may be sought, it is difficult to obtain and when obtained is frequently too old to be of use. The continuous increase in mobility of fire and speed of movement reduces the time during which any given information is of value. Improvement in means of collecting information has not compensated for this shortening of time. The intelligence officer must therefore exercise a continuous supervision and coordination over the search for additional information.

(2) *Information desired.*—The information desired varies with the size of the unit and with the development of the situation during operations. Depending upon the situation, the following factors are of varying importance:

(a) *Distance between opposing forces.*—The distance between opposing forces and the local conditions will show with what elements the enemy can engage and will indicate in a general way the line of contact under various lines of action which he may adopt.

(b) *Enemy activities.*—The enemy's ground and air activities, including movements of combat elements and of service elements and supplies, entrenching, fire, and radio and other communication, furnish information bearing on the enemy's capabilities. Information as to movements should include strength, composition, direction, and location of heads of columns at a specified time.

(c) *Enemy dispositions.*—Information of the location and strength of the hostile position and the dispositions thereon furnishes, either directly or indirectly, indications as to enemy capabilities. The locations of the mass of reserves and of the mass of field artillery are usually of particular importance. Other items may include the location, number, and strength of front line units; deployment of field artillery in width and depth; strength and type of field artillery; location of cavalry forces; location and capacity of airdromes; enemy aviation activity over the area; location and strength of mechanized units; location, amount, and activity of antiaircraft artillery; enemy radio activity; enemy reserves with position, strength, and composition, and the time required to enter action; the distant reinforcements capable of intervening, with strength and composition; and the enemy logistical arrangements with location of installations, important supply centers, and sensitive points on the lines of communication.

(*d*) *Means available to the enemy.*

1. *Manpower.*—A study of the enemy order of battle, by which is meant a study of enemy manpower, location, strength, composition, training, and morale of all enemy troop units, both in line and in reserve, and the ability and character of the enemy commanders, will facilitate an understanding of the enemy's capabilities. This study will be initiated by GHQ at the outbreak of hostilities.

2. *Matériel and supply.*—Knowledge of the type, condition, capacity, and quantity of materiel available to the enemy, particularly of weapons and of transportation and the adequacy or inadequacy of his supply, especially of munitions, will similarly facilitate an estimate of the enemy's capabilities. The presence of bridging materials may have an important and direct bearing on these capabilities in some situations.

(*e*) *Enemy defensive measures.*—Defensive measures of the enemy furnish important evidence of his present attitude and of his capabilities to persist therein or to change to some other line of action. He may supplement natural obstacles with prepared obstacles intended to deny or obstruct our maneuver or to facilitate his own. The following items should be investigated:

1. *Organization of the ground.*—Successive lines of defense, supporting positions and communication, depth of the defensive position, and echelonment of positions.

2. *Strength of organization.*—Organized field works, their type and degree of completion; wire entanglements, shelters, gun emplacements, observation posts, command posts, and communication; and antitank and antiaircraft defensive measures.

3. *Demolitions.*—Location, extent, and nature of all demolitions on roads, bridges, and railways.

4. *Inundations.*—Location of flooded areas or of areas that may be flooded.

5. *Gas.*—Location and extent of areas contaminated with gas, including the nature of the contaminating agent.

(*f*) Other items of information may be required in particular situations.

■ 14. COLLECTING AGENCIES.—*a.* Collecting agencies available to a combat unit vary with its size, facilities, and distance from the front. The battalion is the smallest unit provided with intelligence personnel. It collects its information mainly by means of patrols, scouts, observation posts, reports of front line companies, and the hasty examination of prisoners of war, enemy deserters, inhabitants, and documents. At the other extreme is the army or GHQ, which has at its disposal such facilities as aviation for visual and photographic reconnaissance, radio interception, radio goniometry, secret agents, and sound and flash ranging. The organic collecting agencies of each combat unit are prescribed by appropriate Tables of Organization. Additional collecting agencies may be attached to units which are operating alone.

b. Information collecting agencies available in a combat unit may include part or all of the following:

(1) *Military intelligence personnel.*—This personnel, directly under the orders of the intelligence officer, is assigned to units for the sole duty of conducting intelligence activities which may include—

(*a*) *Installation and operation of an observation service.* In addition to ground observation maintained by troop units themselves, intelligence personnel may establish and maintain supplemental observation of the enemy within the zone of action of the unit.

(*b*) *Mission of intelligence scouts.*—The sole mission of intelligence scouts, either when operating alone or in conjunction with reconnaissance patrols or raiding parties, is to gather information. They engage in combat only in furtherance of this mission.

(*c*) *Examination of prisoners of war, deserters, repatriates, and inhabitants.*— Proper examination of prisoners of war, deserters, repatriates, and inhabitants furnishes valuable and accurate information concerning the enemy order of battle, organization, dispositions, plans and preparations, morale, and numerous other subjects. Specially trained interpreters of the intelligence service conduct the examination.

(d) *Examination of captured documents.*—This study furnishes valuable information relative to the enemy order of battle, troop movements, economic conditions, tactical doctrine, morale, and other subjects. Systematic examination of captured documents of both a personal and official nature is a function of specially trained intelligence personnel. At times they may be assisted by Signal Corps specialists in cryptography.

(e) *Examination of captured matériel.*—Examination of captured matériel by qualified experts enables our forces to keep an accurate check on new developments and eventually leads to the adoption of new technique, tactical doctrine, or matériel to meet these developments.

(f) *Liaison.*—Close liaison with higher, lower, and adjacent units by means of special agents, particularly during battle, facilitates the rapid transmittal of information vital to the commander concerned. Units which have Air Corps organizations assigned or attached for reconnaissance or observation will establish branch intelligence offices with these organizations for the purpose of facilitating the flow of information. The liaison officer in charge will keep constantly informed of the enemy situation and of the essential elements of information by means of close and frequent contact with the G-2 section of higher headquarters. Based upon his knowledge of the situation, he will interview pilots and observers upon the completion of missions with the object of developing and transmitting all possible information.

(g) *Study of aerial photographs.*—The study of aerial photographs by qualified specialists frequently furnishes detailed information of the greatest value concerning the enemy's activities.

(h) *Study of hostile and neutral press.*—This study furnishes important information bearing on enemy resources, political conditions, and morale, as well as information concerning recruiting, troop movements, and other subjects, even though censorship may be applied.

(i) *Espionage.*—Secret agents sometimes procure accurate information of vital importance in the conduct of operations. However, information from this source will require the most careful analysis and evaluation to determine its reliability.

(2) *Troops.*—(*a*) It is the continuing duty of every combat unit to secure all possible information of the enemy and to report such information to higher and affected adjacent commands with the least possible delay. In the absence of positive information, negative information should be reported. In addition to this continuing duty, intelligence missions may be assigned to troop units, directing them to gain certain definite information required by the commander.

(*b*) In addition to the collection of documents found on enemy dead and on prisoners, arrangements should be made for the collection of all printed matter or manuscripts found in places lately occupied by the enemy. Immediately following occupation of a town or village, steps should be taken to seize vacated enemy headquarters, post and telegraph offices, telephone exchanges, police stations, and government and municipal offices in order to prevent the destruction of valuable documents and records.

(*c*) Troop units maintain continuous observation over areas immediately to the front by means of ground observation and by aerial observation when aviation is available. Visual observation should be supplemented by aerial photographs when possible.

(*d*) It is frequently necessary to engage in combat for the specific purpose of obtaining information.

(3) *Special information services of component units of command.*—These services are in general technical and are frequently operated primarily in the interest of the arms to which they pertain. They are not under direct supervision of the intelligence section. However, closest cooperation and liaison are maintained between these agencies and the intelligence section which should be furnished with all information procured. These services include—

(*a*) *Field artillery intelligence section.*—Each echelon of command in the Field Artillery from the battalion up is provided with a staff section charged with intelligence matters and which operates in close coordination with all other similar sections. The general sources of information available to these sections are liaison sections with infantry battalions in contact; field artillery observation posts; balloons working with the artillery; observation aviation on field artillery missions; and observation battalions, sound and flash ranging.

(b) *Air Corps intelligence.*—In addition to normal intelligence activities, the Air Corps produces aerial photographs for intelligence and mapping purposes and prepares and disseminates meteorological data.

(c) *Antiaircraft intelligence service.*—The antiaircraft intelligence service employs observation and special instruments for the detection of aircraft.

(d) *Signal intelligence work.*—In the army and higher headquarters, the signal intelligence service includes telegraph and telephone listening stations, radio interception and goniometry, and laboratories for the solution of codes and ciphers and secret inks.

(e) *Engineer intelligence.*—In addition to normal intelligence activities, the engineers collect data for preparation or correction of maps and in stabilized situations operate a listening service for the detection of mining by the enemy.

(f) *Aircraft warning service.*

c. Higher and adjacent units frequently have means for collecting information not available in a particular unit. Close liaison should be established with these organizations for the purpose of obtaining all pertinent information.

d. The adaptation of new scientific developments to war is gradually making the task of G-2 more complex; at the same time, however, it affords him additional means for the collection of information. Every new invention that may possibly be used as an information gathering or transmitting device should be tested immediately for this purpose.

■ 15. INTELLIGENCE PLAN.—The essential elements of information having been announced, it is necessary that definite and precise instructions for obtaining the required information be given to the collecting agencies or that higher or adjacent headquarters be requested to furnish it. To avoid any possibility of omission or conflict, the intelligence officer must follow a logical, orderly mental process in analyzing and transforming the essential elements of information into missions in allotting the missions to collecting agencies, and in designating the time when and the place where information is to be reported. The scope of the intelligence plan depends upon the sphere of action of the commander for whom it is drawn. It will be subsequently modified to conform to new decisions made by the commander during the development of the situation. A form for use and the steps necessary in the preparation of the intelligence plan are given below.

INTELLIGENCE (G-2) PLAN

Phases or period of the operation	Essential elements of infor- mation	Analysis of essential elements of infor- mation	Collecting agency or other source	Specific orders or requests	Hour and destination at which informa- tion to be reported

a. *Phases or periods of the operation.*—The plan should be devised for a specific phase of the operation or for a particular time interval. The period should not be so long as to require drastic changes in the essential elements of information before its termination, nor so short as to require frequent changes in missions.

b. *Essential elements of information.*—In this column are listed in brief form the essential elements of information to govern in the projected operations or situation.

c. *Analysis of essential elements of information.*—In this column, G-2 briefly records the results of his analysis of the essential elements of information, setting down items that would be needed to answer the questions asked or implied by the wording of the essential elements. Certain essential elements will require very little analysis by the intelligence officer in order to transform them into suitable reconnaissance missions. If the information to be obtained gives a direct answer to the inquiry contained in an essential element, analysis is unnecessary. Others, however, must be subjected to careful analysis in order to determine what indications must be sought to answer the inquiries contained therein. The object of this analysis is to break down the essential elements into indications of possible enemy action that will furnish the basis for definite reconnaissance missions.

d. Collecting agency or other source.—In this column, G-2 records the agency or agencies to be assigned the mission of collecting information bearing on the indications of enemy action. If the information is to be requested from higher or adjacent units, these sources are also listed. To utilize properly the available collecting agencies in the search for information it is essential that G-2 is thoroughly familiar with their powers and limitations and cooperates closely with G-3.

e. Specific orders or requests.—Having analyzed the essential elements and having recorded the general manifestations or indication corresponding to each plan open to the enemy, G-2 next sets down the specific orders for the collecting agencies and the requests to be made on higher or adjacent units. Each of these agencies is given specific and definite missions in accordance with its characteristics and limitations. It is frequently the case that several agencies may be utilized in establishing one definite fact bearing on an essential element.

f. Hour and destination at which information is to be reported.—From a knowledge of the plan of operations gained by close cooperation with G-3, G-2 determines when and where essential information must be reported in order to be of use to the commander. In determining the time at which information must be available, G-2 is guided by the fact that information arriving too late is of no value, and information arriving in advance of its actual need is likely to be inaccurate at the time when projected operations are undertaken.

■ 16. INSTRUCTIONS TO COLLECTING AGENCIES.—*a. General.*—When approved, the completed intelligence plan forms the basis for orders to all collecting agencies. These orders are either published to the collecting agencies in a field order, in the intelligence annex to a field order, or in fragmentary orders. When combat units are required to execute tactical operations in order to obtain information, their tactical missions only and not details of the information required, will be covered by paragraph 3 of the field order.

b. Intelligence annex.—(1) The intelligence annex may be issued by a division or higher unit when it can be distributed in time to be of use. In it the instructions to each collecting agency are placed together in one paragraph. Even though an annex is to be issued, missions of immediate importance should be given in fragmentary orders to the units concerned and later repeated in the annex, if they have not become obsolete by the time it is published.

(2) A form for the intelligence annex is prescribed in FM 101-5.

The Special Intelligence Service (SIS)

In June 1940, the Federal Bureau of Investigation established a Special Intelligence Service (SIS). It was founded specifically as a counterintelligence organization dedicated to fighting Nazi and pro-Nazi activities in the Americas. President Roosevelt issued a directive on the activities of the SIS in December 1941, the month in which the United States entered the war:

In accordance with previous instructions the Federal Bureau of Investigation has set up a Special Intelligence Service covering the Western Hemisphere, with Agents in Mexico, Central America, South America, the Caribbean, and Canada. Close contact and liaison have been established with the Intelligence officials of these countries.

In order to have all responsibility centered in the Federal Bureau of Investigation in this field, I hereby approve this arrangement and request the heads of all Government Departments and Agencies concerned to clear directly with the Federal Bureau of Investigation in connection with any intelligence work within the sphere indicated.

The Director of the Federal Bureau of Investigation is authorized and instructed to convene meetings of the chiefs of the various Intelligence Services operating in the Western Hemisphere and to maintain liaison with Intelligence Agencies operating in the Western Hemisphere.

A further clarification of SIS duties came in February 1942:

The Special Intelligence Service will obtain, primarily through undercover operations supplemented when necessary by open operations, economic, political, industrial, financial and subversive information. The Special Intelligence Service will obtain information concerning movements, organizations, and individuals whose activities are prejudicial to the interests of the United States.

The SIS agents apprehended nearly 900 Axis spies in the Americas between 1940 and 1946. The SIS was also highly active in monitoring revolutionaries in Cuba, the information they gleaned going on to inform post-war U.S. policy towards the island.

★★★

[. . .]

Section VIII
MILITARY INTELLIGENCE TRAINING

■ 32. Basic Principle.—Military intelligence training in all echelons of command will include instructions in the collection, recording, evaluation, and interpretation of information of the enemy and the terrain, in dissemination of military intelligence, in various means of concealing information of our own capabilities or intentions, and in measures to be taken to prevent the enemy from influencing our actions by means of propaganda.

■ 33. Responsibility.—*a. The commander.*—The commanding officer is responsible for intelligence training within his command, and that all officers and enlisted men have an understanding of their military intelligence duties. In battalions and higher organizations, he is assisted in carrying out this responsibility by an assistant chief of staff, G-2.

b. The assistant chief of staff, G-2.—The assistant chief of staff, G-2, is directly responsible for the training of his intelligence section and when directed by the commanding officer, for the supervision of the training of intelligence sections of all subordinate echelons of command. He collaborates with the assistant chief of staff, G-3, in preparation of training programs and makes recommendations. regarding intelligence matters for inclusion therein.

■ 34. Application.—*a.* Training in military intelligence will not be restricted to personnel assigned to the military intelligence sections of various headquarters. Appropriate instruction in this subject will be given to all officers and enlisted men because every officer and enlisted man has a part to play in military intelligence. Personnel assigned to intelligence duties at the various headquarters will be given additional and more thorough instruction appropriate to its assignment. This section deals more in detail with the training of this personnel in the Infantry. With appropriate modifications and additions, it is applicable to all arms and services.

b. Some of the arms and services are charged with activities of immediate importance in military intelligence. These arms and services are responsible for preparation of detailed training programs and instruction of specialists for performance of these duties.

■ 35. QUALIFICATIONS OF PERSONNEL.—Only officers and enlisted men who have a good general military background should be considered for specialized intelligence training. If it is impossible to secure this type of personnel, officers and men will be selected for intelligence duty only after they have completed a course in basic military instruction.

a. Officers.—The assistant chief of staff, G-2, should be thoroughly instructed and trained in the organization, tactics, and logistics of the unit to which he pertains. He is in effect the specialist in the enemy's operations at our headquarters, and he should be the best qualified officer available. An understanding of the enemy's organization, tactical methods, methods of supply, national psychology and language, and a thorough grounding in all military intelligence matters will complete his professional equipment.

b. Enlisted men.—Enlisted men selected for intelligence duty should be of excellent physique, good judgment, observant mind, and possess initiative, imagination, zeal, energy, and a keen sense of responsibility. They should have the equivalent of a high-school education, and should be capable of expressing themselves clearly and of writing a legible hand. In addition to these personal qualifications, they should be trained soldiers before their special intelligence training is begun.

■ 36. METHOD.—*a.* Specialized intelligence training is best accomplished by centralized instruction. The basic training unit is the regiment, which should include an intelligence school in its program of instruction. This school should be conducted by the regimental intelligence officer. The regularly assigned intelligence personnel and selected men detailed from battalions and companies will undergo the course of instruction.

b. The course should contain both theoretical and practical instruction. Tests for proficiency should include a practical demonstration of ability to perform the various duties of the intelligence section.

■ 37. REGIMENTAL COURSE OF INSTRUCTION.—*a.* The detailed training program in the regimental intelligence school will include the following subjects:

Military organization.

Object, organization, and description of the intelligence organization from battalion to division, inclusive.

Collection, recording, evaluation, and interpretation of information.

Dissemination of military intelligence.

Theory and practice of observation, including recognition and appreciation of what is of military value; rendering of accurate, clear, concise, and relevant reports; orientation of the map on the terrain and ready identification of visible terrain features; and establishment and operation of observation posts.

Installation and operation of field telephones.

Use of the compass, field glasses, and simple stereoscope.

Conventional signs, military symbols, and abbreviations.

Map and aerial photograph reading.

Sketching.

Examination and filing of aerial photographs.

Allowance, requisition, distribution, use, and care of maps.

Keeping the situation map and the preparation of overlays.

Verbal and written reports and messages.

Examination of enemy personnel, repatriates, captured documents, and matériel.

Identification of the enemy's uniform, distinctive markings and habits.

Counterintelligence measures, including secrecy discipline; preparation and use of documents; signal communication security; movements of troops and individuals; censorship; and counterpropaganda.

Identification of aircraft.

Scouting and patrolling dismounted.

Visual signaling.

Cross-country movements by day and by night.

Camouflage, camouflage discipline, and the art of concealment.

Means of communication.

Appearance and forms of activity of different arms of the service.

Elementary tactical instruction.

b. Training should not end with completion of the regimental intelligence school, but should be continued and perfected by repetition. In active operations, rest periods should be utilized to correct deficiencies, improve efficiency of the intelligence section, and complete the training of replacements.

■ 38. DIVISIONAL COURSE OF INSTRUCTION.—When the division is assembled as a unit or its various elements are in close proximity to, each other, a divisional school should be established under direct supervision of the assistant chief of staff, G-2. This course should precede he regimental course and should include instruction for all officers and senior noncommissioned officers of the division assigned to intelligence duties on the following subjects:

Organization and duties of the intelligence sections, from battalion to GHQ inclusive.

Organization and operation of the regimental and divisional intelligence office.

Maintenance and use of the regimental and divisional intelligence records.

Ground reconnaissance and observation.

Artillery intelligence sections.

Signal intelligence.

Examination of enemy personnel, repatriates, documents, and matériel at the various echelons of command.

Enemy order of battle.

Topographic engineers, including requisition and issue of maps within the division.

Aerial reconnaissance, including visual observation and aerial photography (flights to be made by the officers).

Coordination of aerial photography and tactical interpretation of aerial photographs.

Terrain studies intended to familiarize the student with effect of terrain upon operations, military resources of the theater of operations, engineer information to be gained from a knowledge or view of the country, and use of foreign maps.

Meteorological information and influence of weather conditions upon operations.

Use of ground and cover.

Counterintelligence measures within the division.

Camouflage, camouflage discipline, and the art of concealment and deception.

U.S. Navy personnel in the Pacific undergo the painstaking work of composing dozens of aerial photographs into a wider landscape. (National Museum of the U.S. Navy)

Identification of aircraft.

Publicity and propaganda.

Tactics and characteristics of weapons of the various arms.

Lectures on appropriate foreign armies and countries, with the object of developing points of strength and weakness of each.

■ 39. MANEUVERS.—Practical training in military intelligence prior to actual operations is extremely difficult. If any degree of proficiency is to be maintained, it is imperative that careful consideration is given the subject in the preparation and execution of maneuvers, particularly two-sided maneuvers. Intelligence measures that may be actively employed include visual and photographic aerial reconnaissance; ground reconnaissance by combat elements; ground observation; signal intelligence, including surveillance of our own communication, and the interception of communication of the opposing side; supervision in all units of security arrangements for the safeguarding of military information; use of camouflage and camouflage discipline; restrictions on use of lights; identification of aircraft; preparation and distribution of aerial photographs as supplements to maps; policies regarding maps to be used and map allowances; requisition and distribution of maps; reception and supervision of visitors; and publicity. The last two measures should, under no circumstances, be allowed to divert the attention of the assistant chief of staff, G-2, from other and more important duties.

■ 40. GHQ INTELLIGENCE SCHOOL.—Success of the intelligence service as a whole will depend in large measure upon selection of suitable personnel and their proper training. The GHQ or theater commander may establish an intelligence school for instruction of selected personnel. Officers detailed to this school who fail to measure up to the highest standards should be promptly relieved. The school should include practical instruction in various military intelligence activities and detailed instruction on the enemy country and army.

CHAPTER 2

Combat and Human Intelligence

World War II saw the rise of increasingly advanced intelligence technologies, especially in the spheres of communications monitoring, cryptanalysis and cryptography, aerial reconnaissance, and radar analysis. Yet at the frontlines, the everyday practice of combat intelligence still depended heavily on the human senses of sight and sound, collecting as much relevant information as possible simply through the practice of attentive observation. That personal observation was still crucial to intelligence-gathering is clear from the fact that an entire War Department volume, FM 30-10, Basic Field Manual, Military Intelligence: Observation, *was dedicated to the principles and techniques of this topic.*

At the outset, the manual makes clear that there is a world of difference between a general observer, such as we all are, and a trained observer, someone whose powers of sight and memory are guided strictly by the operational imperatives, and with a keen eye for seeing and noting everything without rushing to judgments about what was relevant or not. The observer was no island unto himself. As the field manual noted, "Effective observation requires the cooperation of every echelon and every means at the disposal of the commander"—observers worked in close cooperation with each other and with many types of intelligence sources, as the information each person gleaned might only acquire importance when seen in situ with all other pieces of the jigsaw. Army intelligence observers could be found almost anywhere on the battlefront: in an armored vehicle, a frontline trench, a dedicated observation post, an artillery position, amongst an infantry company. They could also be airborne, particularly aboard L-4 Grasshoppers, nimble light aircraft that, from 1942, became organic to Army divisions and artillery groups, primarily for artillery air control but with about 30 percent of their time given to aerial intelligence duties. Few soldiers would have had a more rounded view of the battlefield than the intelligence observers.

★★★

From FM 30-10, *Basic Field Manual, Military Intelligence: Observation* (1940)

SECTION II
CAPABILITIES AND LIMITATIONS
OF OBSERVATION AGENCIES

■ 5. ENUMERATION OF AGENCIES.—Observation is effected by the following agencies:

a. Unit commander in person and his staff officers.

b. Aviation.

c. Troop units in contact with the enemy.

d. Special intelligence personnel from ground observation posts.

e. Field artillery observers and sound and flash ranging stations of the field artillery observation battalions.

f. Antiaircraft artillery intelligence service.

g. Seacoast artillery observation stations.

h. Aircraft warning service.

i. Radio intercept and position-finding sections of the signal intelligence service.

j. Engineer reconnaissance agencies.

k. Weather service.

l. Special observation posts, such as antimechanized defense and gas-warning sentinels.

■ 6. PERSONAL OBSERVATION BY COMMANDER AND HIS STAFF OFFICERS.—*a.* (1) The commander of a unit larger than a battalion will seldom find a ground observation post that affords a view of his entire combat area; however, he must study the terrain over which his troops are to be engaged with the enemy. This will usually require a reconnaissance in person, assisted by certain members of his staff. This reconnaissance may be made from several ground observation posts, or, in appropriate cases, from the air.

(2) In certain situations air observation will furnish the best, and sometimes the only, means to obtain a good general view of the area that is likely to be the scene of operations. Commanders and staff officers must have sufficient experience in air observation so that they may take full advantage of opportunities.

b. Usually the commander will wish to follow the course of the combat, especially at critical periods or in important areas. For this purpose a suitable observation post will be sought that has good means of signal communication and that is conveniently located with respect to the command post. Adequate measures must be taken to conceal the observation post and to insure its security against surprise raids.

c. When he has personal observation, the commander is able to evaluate reports with greater assurance. However, he must be on his guard against assigning undue importance to his own observations as compared with reports from other sources or from areas not visible from his own observation post. Otherwise he risks getting a distorted picture of the situation.

[. . .]

■ 8. TROOP UNITS IN DIRECT CONTACT WITH ENEMY.—*a.* Much valuable information about the enemy comes from the observation by troop units in direct contact. Reconnaissance detachments gain first ground contact with the enemy and report their observation by the most rapid means available. Patrols are, in effect, mobile observation posts that advance close to or within the enemy lines and obtain information through their eyes and ears. Constant scrutiny of the hostile dispositions and activities is provided by observers of platoons and companies in the front lines. Platoon sergeants, communication sergeants, buglers, and messengers of rifle units are given special training in observation, but all soldiers of infantry and cavalry rifle units should become proficient in field observation as given in FM 21-45.

b. Troops must be taught that their observation plays an important part in the whole scheme of intelligence and that anything they discover about the enemy should be reported to higher authority. The intelligence picture that is developed at higher headquarters is composed of small items that may seem unimportant to the unit reporting them. The complete picture, however, will enable the commander to formulate his own plan and to counter enemy action and so help the reporting troops themselves.

c. Troops should not expect sensational results from their reports. They may never become aware of the part these reports play in completing the intelligence picture. However, troops should be taught that all reports contribute their part, and that they serve their purpose even if not acknowledged.

d. Troops should be impressed that negative information may be highly important. The fact that no enemy activity is observed in a given area may be a valuable clue to the enemy's capabilities.

e. In the stress of combat it is exceedingly difficult for units in contact to report promptly the results of their observations. These reports may be facilitated if platoon and company commanders are furnished outline forms that may be quickly filled in and sent to the next higher echelon.

f. Observation by engineer reconnaissance parties is usually supplied in the form of engineer reconnaissance reports.

g. Whenever operations are sufficiently stabilized, information from shell fragments should be sought. Troops must be taught that the caliber of hostile artillery firing on any point is important information. Often experienced observers can judge this by the size of shell craters. When practicable, any sizeable shell fragments are gathered and turned over to the nearest artillery command post with exact information on location of shelled area and the time shelling occurred. Duds should be carefully marked and reported. Fuze fragments or rotating bands are of special interest. Whenever gas shells are being used, a sample of gas-contaminated earth from a shell crater, as well as fragments of such shell, should be sent to the rear for examination by the chemical field laboratory and identification of the gas used.

h. Information of enemy chemical warfare means and methods may sometimes have great importance. Samples of enemy chemical agents, captured chemical weapons, and gas masks are obtained by the unit gas officers and sent through the division chemical officer. Reports of observation of the enemy's chemical warfare activities are transmitted through intelligence channels.

i. Enemy messages, codes, cipher devices and keys, signal operation instructions, circuit diagrams, etc., taken from prisoners, casualties, or captured in raids, from pigeons, or after abandonment by the enemy may be extremely valuable and should be physically transmitted without delay.

■ 9. SPECIAL INTELLIGENCE PERSONNEL AT GROUND OBSERVATION POSTS.—*a.* Ground observation posts cover the terrain in depth. Their areas of responsibility include those of the units in contact; they reinforce the observation of their subordinate echelons. Areas that are defiladed from one post can often be observed from other positions. As soon as the situation becomes sufficiently stabilized, a coordinated plan should be made by each intelligence officer to secure maximum results from his own observers and from those of subordinate units. The observation net operates continuously, day and night. During periods of rapid movements, information about the enemy is sought especially on the following points:

Location of advanced elements.

Emplacements of automatic weapons, antitank guns, and chemical weapons.

Location of observation and command posts.

Artillery positions.

Tank obstacles and traps.

Movements of troops.

Location of supply points.

Friendly areas subject to aerial attack or observation or contaminated with persistent gas.

b. When fronts stabilize for more than a few days, observers obtain information on the following points:

Daily routine of the enemy.

Hours of relief and supply.

Routes frequently used.

Emplacements of weapons of any type.

Works such as trenches, obstacles, and observation and command posts.

Use of visual and sound communication, including the signals used and their probable meanings as evidenced by enemy actions following the signals.

At all times, forward areas held by friendly troops are kept under observation. Location of friendly advanced elements are particularly noted. Any signals made by them are promptly relayed.

c. Every ground observation post needs the following items as basic equipment:

Field glasses or telescope.

Instrument for measuring angles (aiming circle, *BC*-telescope, prismatic or lensatic compass, etc.).

Watch.

Map, sketch, or photograph of terrain under observation.

Material for recording observations, including journal and special report forms, overlay paper, and colored pencils.

Means of signal communication with command post, preferably telephone.

When the situation stabilizes and observation posts become more completely organized, the following equipment may be added:

Range finders.

Periscopes.

Higher power telescopes.

Additional maps and aerial photographs.

Panoramic sketches and range cards.

Map or plotting boards.

Alternate means of signal communication.

d. Certain factors reduce the effectiveness of ground observation.

(1) Some areas are certain to be defiladed from even the best observation post.

(2) Rain, fog, and darkness limit observation.

(3) Shifting back and forth of the front line reduces the effectiveness of advanced observation posts.

(4) An observation post located by the enemy may become ineffective, because the enemy may conceal his activities in the field of vision or he may neutralize the observation post by fire or smoke.

e. The selection and organization of ground observation posts are covered in section IV.

f. The number of favorable points of observation is limited in many types of terrain. Unless the commander coordinates their use, there is likely to be a congestion of observing parties that will offer fruitful targets to the enemy's artillery or aerial attack and may disclose the plan of action. In the initial stages of contact, it may be difficult or undesirable to control the use of observation posts too closely; however, areas available for selection of observation posts should be indicated in advance whenever possible, so that there may be a minimum of shifting during action, and an opportunity to install signal communication. As the situation develops, intelligence officers must be constantly on the alert to recommend adjustments in observation posts that will insure most complete coverage of the entire battlefield and also reduce the congestion of certain areas.

g. (1) Observation posts must be carefully camouflaged. When a post is to be constructed in a system of field fortification, it should not be at the same location as the temporary observation post used during the initial stages of battle. The new location should be far enough from the old one so that it will not be neutralized by artillery fire directed at the former location. The erection of camouflage must precede the construction.

(2) The mere fact that an enemy does not fire on an observation post does not insure that he is in ignorance of its location. He may have the post spotted and may intend to neutralize or destroy it at critical phases of the battle. Hence every observation post should have an alternate location that is able to cover approximately the same field and that has an alternate means of signal communication available.

h. In order to preserve the secrecy of observation posts, all military personnel must be made to observe the following precautions:

(1) Only intelligence or signal communication personnel and individuals authorized by the unit commander or higher authority should be permitted to visit an observation post.

(2) Authorized persons approaching or departing from an observation post should use the utmost care to avoid disclosing its location.

(3) No form of transportation should stop near an observation post.

(4) Trails are plainly visible on aerial photographs. Hence every effort should be made to prevent the development of new trails or paths leading to or from an observation post. Only marked and established trails should be used.

(5) Fires, smoking, lights, loud talking, and any unnecessary noise should be prohibited.

i. (1) If the maps available do not have sufficient names for easy reference, the division G-2 may give designations to important features, such as hills, woods, and road intersections in the division area. These designations are furnished all observation elements.

(2) As soon as possible, infantry regiments and supporting artillery units determine the accurate location of their observation posts and their positions relative to each other. These locations are furnished the division G-2, who causes them to be communicated to the intelligence sections of all units in the division.

(3) As soon as these coordinated observation posts, together with the location of principal reference points, are available, observation reports can be quickly transmitted in the following form:

> Observation post (may be designated by code name over the telephone).
> Azimuth of object reported.
> Distance in yards.
> Object reported (frontage and depth if appropriate).
> Time observed.
> Any additional details of location.

An example of such a message follows:

"OP Magic one; 270 degrees, 1,500 yards; machine gun; 10:15 AM; east of red barn."

[. . .]

Section III
OBSERVATION IN DIFFERENT PHASES OF BATTLE

■ 18. PRIOR TO BATTLE.—*a.* At the beginning of operations theater headquarters will immediately employ aviation and ground reconnaissance forces for distant reconnaissance. Arrangements will be made for prompt use of radio intelligence and aircraft warning services. Ground observation will be organized on the frontiers.

b. Aviation will seek especially for information about the enemy on the following points: Concentration areas; principal movements of rail and motor transport; detraining zones; bivouac areas; deployment of his aviation; areas being organized for defense; zones being prepared for destruction and demolition.

c. Night reconnaissance will be especially important during this period.

d. The signal intelligence service plays a highly important role at the beginning of operations because in the course of setting up his organization the enemy is likely to disclose important information both by the positions and movements of his radio stations and possibly by careless use of his codes.

e. The aircraft warning service has a most important task in the early phases of operations. Its observation posts are advanced as far as possible and a lookout service is established that includes any permanent observation posts of territorial defense as well as of tactical units at the disposition of the theater commander. Information on hostile air activity is transmitted through the organized information centers with whom G-2 organizes a close system of liaison.

f. (1) From the beginning of mobilization all units must provide for their own close security by means of observation against attacks by hostile air or mechanized forces. If the unit is charged with defense of an area that has a coast line, lake front, or other large water area, provision for observing possible attacks by water must be made. The commander of every large unit in the theater of operations, whether on the march or in bivouac, must provide permanently manned observation posts, even though his unit is at a distance from the enemy. Zones favorable for hostile landings, either of parachute troops or airplanes, and possible routes of approach for mechanized forces are given special attention. Provision is made for gas sentinels.

(2) The commanders of large units allot missions and zones of observation to subordinate echelons. Intelligence observers may be used for surveillance of areas in the vicinity of command posts.

(3) Army commanders provide for the organization of observation in the army rear areas. Commanders of communications zones and zone of

interior areas and installations make provision for observation at critical points in their respective zones.

■ 19. OFFENSIVE OPERATIONS.—*a*. During the approach to battle, aviation and mechanized distant reconnaissance initially furnishes most important observation, but appropriate steps must be taken to provide for prompt employment of all observation agencies as soon as the opposing forces come within their range of action.

b. Aviation seeks out and reports the enemy main forces. Mechanized and cavalry units determine the limits of hostile advance and identify his leading elements. Areas found to be contaminated with persistent gas or mined in preparation for such gassing are promptly reported and posted, thus protecting other friendly units from marching into them without warning. The signal intelligence service locates the hostile command posts and observes their movements; it also intercepts hostile radio communications. The aircraft warning service not only furnishes warning of hostile attacks, but by reporting hostile air activity furnishes G-2 with valuable indications as to the areas to which the enemy is giving greatest attention; this may be a factor in determining the enemy's capabilities. If the air situation permits, observation balloons may be utilized whenever the situation becomes sufficiently stable to make their employment worthwhile. Consideration is given to the possible loss of surprise by use of balloons.

c. During the advance to battle, axes of march are frequently designated along which the ground observation of mobile units is advanced by bounds. These axes of observation are integrated with the movements of advance guards and main bodies so that the whole zone of the advance is covered as completely as possible with an observation net.

d. Special observation agencies whose installation requires a certain delay, such as the artillery observation units, aircraft warning service, and certain signal intelligence units, may be held initially in reserve; however, advance echelons of these agencies are pushed forward to the extreme limit of advance, protected, if necessary, by special security detachments. This enables these agencies to accelerate their entry into action and to furnish the results of their observations in time to be of value to the commander in planning his battle.

e. As soon as contact is established, the observation network developed during the approach march is reinforced. When the enemy is defending a position, observation continues to operate as during the approach march. All agencies concentrate their efforts on determining the details of position and the dispositions of the enemy. The observation service concentrates on securing information that will aid the commander in preparation for an attack.

f. When in contact with an enemy in superior force who continues to advance aggressively, the complete system of ground observation is deployed on the position selected by the commander for his principal resistance. The observation agencies concentrate on following the deployment of the hostile forces and seek to determine the probable directions of the enemy's main effort as indicated by his attack dispositions. The establishment of the observation system is given high priority in the organization of the defense.

g. The system of ground observation is advanced by echelons as the attack progresses.

h. There is always danger of congestion on prominent points and consequent destruction of means of observation by hostile artillery fire or air attack. To prevent this the commander may designate certain axes of observation along which subordinate units will move their observation posts.

i. During pursuit and exploitation, observation is used in the same general manner as in the approach march.

j. An attack against a prepared position or a zone defense requires a careful and detailed preparation. The observation service plays an important part in this preparation. It may be necessary to limit the amount of air and balloon observation in order to attain surprise.

■ 20. DEFENSIVE OPERATIONS.—*a.* Observation is of particular importance in defensive operations. Observation posts remain in position for considerable periods; the exact locations of the posts can be determined with great precision. The enemy is apt to disclose important information by variations in the routine he has established. The locations of new batteries and new dumps of munitions and matériel are hard to camouflage completely. The observation system must cover the battlefield completely and continuously so that in spite of the enemy's efforts to screen his activities our intelligence system will have the indications that will permit a determination of the enemy's capabilities.

b. Reports on hostile air activity are of particular importance in defense. Reports of observation and photographic flights, areas, and times at which the enemy furnishes pursuit protection, and areas subjected to hostile air attack are all reported by the ground observation posts and troop observers as well as by the antiaircraft observers and the aircraft warning service.

c. Any indications of employment of tanks or emplacements of chemical mortars are of special importance.

d. Units charged with the defense of unusually wide frontages give special attention to organizing their observation. In order to economize troops, many areas will depend chiefly on observation for their protection. Dependence will be placed upon fire or reserves to meet any enemy movement through these areas. The observation agencies of some of the units held in reserve may be called upon to cover some of the areas in which their troops may later be employed. However, no reserve unit should be completely stripped of its organic observation because it may have to operate unexpectedly in another area. Special attention must be given to providing for the prompt transmission of information gained.

■ 21. SPECIAL OPERATIONS.—*a. Operations at night or in fog.*—Observation is of special importance at times of low visibility. Particular attention must be given to sound-ranging and to listening posts during these periods. Dusk and dawn require special alertness at all observation posts. Visual observers can often obtain quite accurate information at night, especially as to the direction of lights observed. Inasmuch as fog may lift unexpectedly, all observation posts must remain on the alert during such periods, in the hope of surprising the enemy in some movement he hopes to conceal.

b. Combat in woods.—The short fields of vision available in this type of battle compel special measures by observers. Personal reconnaissance is facilitated because movement is camouflaged by the woods. In the attack, observation post locations are sought at the edges of the woods, in clearings, and in more open portions. In the defense, arrangements are made to improve the field of vision. In dense woods listening posts are established.

c. *Mountain operations.*—(1) The following special conditions apply in this type of battle:

(a) Fields of vision are likely to be extensive, but to contain many defiladed areas.

(b) Atmospheric conditions are subject to extreme and often sudden variations; fog and mist may be followed quickly by very clear weather.

(c) The noise of streams and effects of echoes may be very deceptive as to source of sounds.

(d) The character of the terrain and the fields of vision may change abruptly in very short distances.

(2) The following measures may be used to overcome observation difficulties in mountain operations:

(a) Increase in observation personnel, especially on the defense and when on extended fronts.

(b) Careful coordination of all means of observation; use of special posts on lower levels combined with those on high points.

(c) Maximum use of aerial photographs, both verticals and obliques.

(d) Use of natural shelters for observation posts, both for camouflage and for protection.

(e) Special attention by observation agencies to defiles and routes through which movements must be made; provision for general surveillance and air patrol of impassable areas.

(3) For signal communication in mountainous areas, full use must be made of visual and radio means. Wire lines are difficult to lay and to maintain.

Section IV
OBSERVATION POSTS

■ 22. Selection.—a. The selection of sites for observation posts will be influenced by the degree of mobility of the operations. In rapidly moving situations, the post must be hastily selected and frequently moved. In periods of slower movement, the location may be selected more deliberately. The site selected for an observation post should be that point within the sector of the unit concerned from which the best view of the terrain toward the enemy and in rear of his front lines can be secured, and which at the same time is sheltered from his view. An ideal site will afford an excellent and unobstructed view to such a distance as will afford ample warning of an enemy advance; it will be completely sheltered from the view of the enemy's observers, both ground and aerial; and the approaches to it will be such as to render it easily accessible and permit individuals to come and go without being seen by the enemy.

b. Care must be taken that observation over the entire front is provided for. At times a unit will lack good observation over a part of its front because of a hill, a deep ravine, or woods, but effective observation may be possible from the area of an adjacent unit. This may be covered by cooperation between units by having the adjacent unit cover this part of the front or by arranging for the first unit to place an observation post in the adjacent unit's territory to provide observation behind the obstacle. An observation post should, if practicable, be within easy reach of the command post, but the two should always be separated by such a distance as will prevent the activities of the one from interfering with the special functions of the other and insure against one's being caught in fire directed at the other. Alternate positions should be selected.

c. Frequently the military crest of a hill is the best site for an observation post. Observers may be required to establish themselves in trees, towers, and houses. Often satisfactory observation posts will be found on side slopes rather than crests. Side positions are usually easier to conceal and to approach from the rear. In stabilized operations the best available site may be in some portion of the trench system, but an observation post should be so placed only when there is no other site practicable, as the constant passage of men along the trenches will probably operate to divert the attention of the observers.

d. Before and during an advance or an attack, successive sites for new observation posts must be tentatively selected. These should possess as many as possible of the qualities mentioned above, and should be within the zone of advance of the unit. The same procedure will apply in the event of a retrograde movement.

e. When the unit is engaged in an advance or an attack, the necessity for continuous observation requires the "leapfrogging" of observation posts. Careful arrangements are required in order that while one observing group is moving, another may be able to remain constantly in observation of the enemy and of the terrain toward him.

■ 23. CONSTRUCTION.—*a.* An observation post in open warfare will ordinarily be but a point on the terrain with the use of some natural camouflage, such as grass and leaves, as an aid to concealment and the removal of obstructions which interfere with the observers' view. Construction, under most favorable conditions, will be limited to rough shelter from rifle and machine-gun fire. Until the operations become stabilized, the hasty preparation of selected points for use as observation posts is made by the intelligence personnel concerned.

b. When troops remain in the same position for longer periods, there will be sufficient time and necessity for carefully constructed observation posts. New sites are chosen and carefully camouflaged before construction begins. More elaborate provisions are made for concealment, for protection against artillery fire and bombing, and for the convenience of the observing group.

c. The construction of observation posts of more or less permanent type is supervised by intelligence officers, but the actual work is done by details from other troops. Intelligence personnel should have a thorough understanding of the fundamentals applying to the construction and camouflage of permanent observation posts.

■ 24. OPERATION.—*a.* The observation post is allotted a definite area or sector to be covered by its observation. This sector is marked on the map furnished the observing group, and its limits should be clearly understood by every member of the group. If but one observation post is to be established by the unit, the sector extends laterally, for a short distance into the terrain in front of the units on the right and left. If the unit is operating alone or on an exposed flank, the sector extends laterally for a distance sufficient to prevent a surprise attack against the exposed flank or flanks. If two or more observation posts are to be established, the sectors allotted to them overlap to an extent that will insure effective observation of all terrain with which the unit is concerned. Sometimes an observing group is directed to observe and report upon ground in front of another unit, which cannot be covered by the latter's observation; in this case the particular ground must be clearly marked on the map.

b. Detailed recording and routine transmittal of information are more or less impracticable when troops are on the move and during periods of special activity. If accurate information is secured and transmitted to the command post in time to be of value, the details of operation are of minor importance.

c. Observing group.—When the observation post is to be operated for more than a few hours it should consist of not less than four men. As the performance of their duties involves considerable strain, observing groups are relieved every 24 hours, when practicable. In stabilized or semistabilized operations an observing group may have to remain at its post for several days; in this case arrangements for food and water are necessary. Men actually engaged in observing cannot maintain their alertness more than about 2 hours. Better results will be obtained if the observer and recorder exchange places at intervals of about 30 minutes. The pair is then relieved every 2 hours. If the group is not equipped with a telephone, one or two additional men may be attached to it for messenger service, or those not actually on watch may be used for this purpose.

d. Posting the group.—(1) Upon arrival at the selected site, the group leader immediately posts one or more men in observation of the sector allotted him. He then selects the exact point to be occupied by his observation post, orients his map, marks his location thereon, and arranges for the necessary camouflage.

(2) The first step is to locate the position on the map with the greatest accuracy possible, as explained in FM 21-25. A basic orientation line is selected toward some prominent object near the center of the field of vision of the observation post. The magnetic azimuth of this line is recorded and its distance noted. The magnetic azimuth readings and distances of other important reference points on the terrain are then noted.

(3) These data are registered on a range card and furnish the basic means by which the observer can quickly locate and report any object in his field of vision. The coordinates of the map in use are transposed to the range card to facilitate reference in messages and reports.

(4) With the oriented map before them, all members of the group are made familiar with the terrain to be watched. If necessary, important features are marked on the map, and the group is made thoroughly familiar with their names or special designations.

(5) The group is then divided into reliefs of two men each, designated as the observer and the recorder, respectively. When an observation post is first established it is advisable to assign several men to watching the terrain at the same time; as soon as it becomes apparent that the enemy is not dangerously active, all but one team is relieved. The first relief having been placed on watch, the group leader reports his exact location together with the gist of the enemy information secured. The men not on watch retire far enough to avoid interference with the first relief.

e. Observer.—(1) The observer divides the terrain included in his sector of observation into a series of overlapping zones, the nearest of which takes in the ground just beyond the front line of his unit while the farthest includes the limiting line, in depth, of his sector. He settles himself into a comfortable position, which affords a steady rest for his glasses and from which he can secure an unobstructed view of the sector of observation. He then searches the terrain for indications of enemy activity.

(2) Beginning with the zone nearest him the observer makes a slow and thorough examination of the terrain, searching from one edge of the zone to the other. Proceeding to the examination of the next zone, he searches it in the opposite direction, and he continues in this manner until the whole sector has been examined. If any movement catches the eye, the point where it occurred should be watched closely for a few moments.

(3) The observer searches not only for movements but also for other indications of enemy activity, such as trenches, paths, gun positions, observation posts, and wire.

(4) Having determined the character of the movement or object discovered, the observer locates it on his map and transmits the information at once to the recorder.

f. Recorder.—(1) The recorder accurately records information secured by the observer and operates the telephone.

(2) Information is recorded on blanks furnished for that purpose, on the map, and in the form of sketches. Carbon copies of reports are made in the observer's book and retained at the observation post.

(3) All information secured is recorded. Items that seem of little or no value to the observing group may develop great value when studied by intelligence sections in connection with other information. Recurrences and discontinuances of acts or events already reported upon may be of prime importance. Time, place, and character of action must be accurately noted. When pertinent, such deductions as are warranted by conditions may be included but clearly *as deductions* and not as statements of fact.

(4) The locations of hostile units, trenches, weapons, wire, and observation posts are plotted on the map.

(5) The position of the recorder should be sufficiently close to that of the observer to permit conversation in low tones.

g. Transmittal of information.—(1) If the observation post is equipped with a telephone, information of immediate importance is telephoned to the command post, or if that is impracticable, it is visually signaled or sent by messenger. Especially in situations of rapid movement, prearranged visual signals or code groups may be advantageous for conventional messages such as "Nothing to report," "Enemy in sight," or "Enemy tank approaching." In the use of signaling or radio, special care is necessary to prevent detection. It may be desirable to set up the sending station at some distance from the observation post.

(2) The accumulated observer's reports are sent by messenger periodically (usually twice a day) to the intelligence officer unless they have been of sufficient urgency to be sent by special messenger. An observer's book should be maintained at the observation post in which a carbon copy of the observer's report is kept for reference.

The German Soldier

The Intelligence Bulletin *was a monthly document published by the War Department's Military Intelligence Service. It was distributed to U.S. military personnel only; it was not a civilian publication. The* Intelligence Bulletin *provided the best available information on Axis tactics and weaponry, along with some insight into the enemy's psychology. The following text is from the November 1942 edition, specifically an article entitled "The Individual Soldier." It offers a detailed explanation of the psychology of the German soldier. The first section lays the basic groundwork.*

1. WHAT HE IS LIKE

The German soldier is a grimly determined fighter who has scarcely known what it is like to live as an independent human being, and whose religion may be summed up in a single word: Nazism.

In his parent's home, in school, in the many subdivisions of the Hitler Youth Movement, in the shop, and in the Reich Labor Service, the army recruit has been bred as a National Socialist. The official point of view regarding national and international matters has been the only point of view he has ever known. All his newspapers, books, magazines, and every other source of information available to him have been "doctored." He knows what the Nazi Party permits him to know, and nothing more. Above everything in the world, he is aware of his allegiance to the National Socialist State and of his life work of being a German. It is his proudest belief that he belongs to "the German race" and that as a result he is something he calls an "Aryan."

Nothing is easier to explode than this theory, and the fact that the Germans cling to it shows how far state control has corrupted the common sense of a whole nation. Actually, the Germans are not a separate race. They are Caucasians (as are nearly all European peoples), and since Germany has been the melting pot of all the invading groups which have crossed that territory for the past 3,000 years, German blood is a mixture of many strains. It is heavily Polish, for example.

The truth about the word "Aryan" is that it does not pertain to physical characteristics, but to the science of words, and means a member of one of the peoples who speak what is called an "Indo-European" language; hence Portuguese, Armenians, Greeks, Italians, and dozens of other peoples are as Aryan as the Germans. Contrary to all modern science, however, the Nazis use the term in a racial sense, and identify the German people with it.

The German superiority myth is not an invention of the Nazis, who merely give great publicity to a theory that was popular back in the 19th century.

The Kingdom of Prussia and her sympathizers, at that time struggling to combine numerous German states into a united nation, found the doctrine of racial superiority a powerful political weapon. It must be remembered that the German soldier is a product of 1,500 unhappy years of German history, and that the inability of his people to form a united and lasting state has given him a private sense of national inferiority. In "Aryanism," with the Nazi trimmings, the German people have hit upon a kind of national religion, and one which helps them to forget that as a nation they have always been a political failure. In this religion the leaders are the state, and the state is god.

In teaching German superiority, the soldier's army training more or less picks up where the Youth Movement leaves off. His mind is filled with continuous propaganda which exalts war and makes it seem unavoidable, humane, and heroic. The present war is presented to him as a struggle for national existence forced on Germany by a degenerate, crafty, and ruthless enemy. The soldier is taught this kind of thing hand in hand with his really excellent training in purely military matters--not that he is receiving military training for the first time. It must be remembered that in the activities of Youth Movement societies he learned rifle marksmanship, close-order drill, combat scouting, and many other aspects of warfare. All along the way, these societies were preparing him for a soldier's life.

As soon as he is called up for Service, he is tested for his special abilities and qualifications so that the Army can decide in which branch he is to be trained. He is then sent to a training center, where he remains for about six months, unless the need for troops in the field is so great that his training period must be shortened. At the present time, German training centers take advantage of as many short cuts as possible. Normally, during the soldier's first 4 months at the training center, emphasis is placed on his development as an individual fighter. During the fifth month he works on platoon and company problems, and during the sixth month he takes part in battalion and regimental exercises. After the sixth month his class ordinarily would join in divisional maneuvers, but in wartime such large-scale maneuvers often are omitted. If the recruit displays marked ability while at the training center, he may be allowed to attend a specialists school—for example, a Communications School.

The German soldier's recreation is designed to build up his sense of mental and physical superiority. German sports have been geared to assist the nation-wide program of military training. Their chief function is to toughen the body and encourage combativeness. In most games, as in military training, the emphasis is on the importance of winning—not on sports for their own sake.

Plenty of books and motion pictures are made available to the troops, but, as is so often the case with Nazi generosity, there is a catch. The books are selected, and the films designed, with one fundamental purpose in mind: propaganda. Even when the soldier is relaxing, the doctrine of German superiority is being drummed into him.

The German Army pay scale is lower than ours. A German private receives $6 a month; a lance corporal, $30.80; a corporal, $47.48; a sergeant, $67.20; a first sergeant, $74.72. A lieutenant may receive from $960 to $1,680 annually; a first lieutenant, from $1,360 to $1,680. A private at the front gets an extra 40 cents a day, or 80 cents a day if he is sent to Africa. Officers and noncommissioned officers receive double this amount. Only soldier's dependents who can show evidence that they need assistance are granted financial aid, and even then the matter is in the hands of a district administrative authority. When the families of officers or noncommissioned officers include children, the following monthly allowances are made: $4 when there is one child, $8 if there are two, $10 if there are three or four. Unfortunately for the soldier's family, this does not insure a decent living standard, partly because such basic necessities as food, clothing, and fuel are not only very expensive in the Reich, but dangerously scarce.

Despite the internal conditions in Germany, the average German soldier seldom feels that he is being pushed around by his leaders. His morale is good. He takes pride in the unit to which he belongs, and fights without a word of question or reproach. On the whole, he is convinced that although World War II is unfortunate, it is necessary if his people, the master race, are to rule the world.

★★★

German prisoners of war (POWs) passed through American hands in daunting volumes during World War II. From January to June 1945, for example, some 4.5 million Germans were either captured or surrendered as the Allied forces pushed into Western Germany alone. The prisoners ranged from privates to generals, administrators to war criminals, and thus they presented a potential goldmine of information for U.S. military intelligence operators. What better way to find out actionable facts about the enemy than to ask the enemy himself?

Of course, in reality the extraction of militarily useful information from POWs was a challenging business. As a general rule, the more important

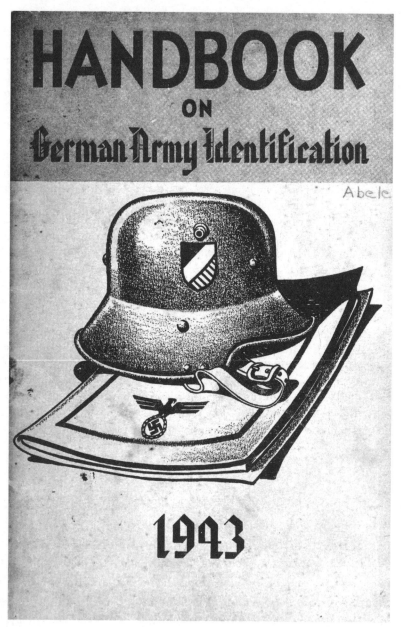

The *Handbook on German Army Identification* was prepared at the Military Intelligence Training Center in Camp Ritchie, Maryland in 1943. It acted as a guide to help U.S. soldiers identify uniforms and ranks in all the German armed services and paramilitary organizations. (USHMM)

A further image from the *Handbook on German Army Identification* showing National Socialist paramilitary insignia. (USHMM)

the person (in which case we are largely referring to officers or senior technical personnel), the less likely they would be to give up their knowledge. Given that the United States prided itself on avoiding the use of "physical coercion" (i.e. torture) in interrogations, which it actually saw as counter-productive and yielding poor-quality intelligence, intelligence officers instead had to draw on psychology, deception, logic, friendship, and all manner of other patient tricks to draw out valuable nuggets of information from their prisoners. Sometimes this was a highly sophisticated operation. At Fort Hunt, Virginia, for example, a clandestine interrogation center (only known by the code name "PO Box 1142") for important German prisoners was established, the building including sophisticated eavesdropping devices to monitor German conversations. At its most basic, however, some valuable information could be extracted from low-ranking Germans just by offering a smile, a cigarette, and reassuring words.

FM 30-15, Basic Field Manual, Military Intelligence: Examination of Enemy Personnel, Repatriates, Documents and Matériel *provided detailed guidance on the intelligence practices and procedures for handling POWs, individually or in large volumes. It also discussed the handling of documentation taken from prisoners or found during the course of operations. Given that this particular edition of the manual was written in 1939, prior to the outbreak of hostilities, the scale of the human intelligence (HUMINT) intelligence challenge ahead of the United States could scarcely yet be envisaged.*

★★★

From FM 30–15, *Basic Field Manual, Military Intelligence: Examination of Enemy Personnel, Repatriates, Documents and Matériel* (1939)

Section II
ENEMY PERSONNEL

5. General—*a.* The provisions of this section are particularly applicable to the examination of prisoners of war but, with suitable modification, may be used as a guide in the examination of all classes of personnel.

b. Prisoners of war are one of the most fruitful sources of information. They are witnesses from within the enemy's lines who have seen and heard. Their systematic and methodical examination is highly important. Enemy civilian personnel are of less importance as a source of information because they are not trained observers. Nevertheless, as a possible source of information they must not be overlooked.

6. Limitations.—*The examination of enemy personnel in the various commands will be strictly limited to those items of immediate importance to the commander concerned.* Early and complete examination of enemy personnel by untrained officers or enlisted men will accomplish no useful purpose and will delay and probably frustrate later examination in the higher commands.

7. Object.—The object of the examination is to determine the enemy's intentions and other information of immediate tactical importance to

A Japanese soldier is interrogated via an interpreter by intelligence officers on New Guinea in 1942. (NARA)

the lower echelons of command, the order of battle, morale, tactical and technical methods of the hostile army, the manpower and economic conditions in the enemy country, and other information of primary importance to the higher command.

8. Qualifications of examiner.—Intelligence personnel who examine prisoners of war should be well grounded in the language, history, political organization, geography, customs, and habits of the hostile country and familiar with the intellectual, economic, financial, political, religious, and social life thereof, and with any racial differences that may exist therein. They should know many details about the various parts of the enemy country, understand the aspirations of the different racial and political groups, be able to converse with prisoners about their trades and occupations, and be capable of using the native dialect and military slang.

a. Military qualifications.—In addition to the general cultural background, the examiner must have a thorough and detailed knowledge of military terms, organization, armament, tactics and methods of combat, logistics, and intelligence methods of the enemy army and of each particular arm and service. To this knowledge of the enemy must be added a profound knowledge of the organization, methods of combat, and intelligence procedure of our own Army.

b. Investigational qualifications.—In addition to general and military qualifications, the examiner must be expert in cross-examination, conscientious, and persevering. He must have a keen insight into the minds of others and, with experience, should acquire a flair and aptitude for his work—qualities upon which depend in large measure the results of examination.

9. Coercion.—*a.* In accordance with the Geneva Convention of 1929, to which the United States subscribed, no coercion may be used on prisoners or other personnel to obtain information relative to the state of their army or country; and prisoners or others who refuse to answer may not be threatened, insulted, or exposed to unpleasant or disadvantageous treatment of any kind. The rules adopted at the Geneva Convention do not prohibit the examination of prisoners or others, and provision will always be made for such examination.

b. Coercion is not the most effective method of obtaining information from prisoners. If an examiner fails to obtain information by such means, as is generally the case, he immediately finds himself in a condition of moral inferiority with respect to the prisoner. A cigarette or a cup of coffee will frequently elicit more accurate and important information than threats. Humane treatment does not imply loss of dignity or lack of military bearing on the part of the examiner; it indicates an understanding of human nature to which the prisoner will generally respond. Placed in the proper frame of mind and aided by a map, chart, or sketch to help orient himself physically and mentally, the average prisoner will talk. False rumor within the enemy ranks concerning brutal treatment of prisoners by our forces will inevitably react to our benefit if humane treatment is accorded them when captured.

10. The examination.—*a.* At each echelon of command, enemy personnel will be examined individually and those examined will be kept separated from those remaining to be examined. When time and facilities permit, a brief of the prisoner's statements will accompany him to the rear for the purpose of assisting the intelligence officers at the higher headquarters in further examination.

b. In the more rapidly moving situations it may be necessary to modify the system of examination prescribed herein. At such times the initiative and ingenuity of all ranks will be taxed to the maximum; nevertheless, information derived from the examination of prisoners must continue to be obtained. It may become necessary to send intelligence officers forward to get the needed information, and plans should be made accordingly. Equally important is getting the information back while maintaining close contact with the advancing units. If wire communication has not been established and radio is not available, use should be made of messengers or carrier pigeons.

c. Examination parallels the system of evacuation.—(1) The examination of enemy military personnel parallels the system of evacuation and constitutes an incident of evacuation. The final examination is conducted by the army at the army prisoner of war enclosure or by theater headquarters at the central prisoner of war enclosure.

(2) Commanders of escorts and prisoner of war installations, and commanders of medical installations and graves registration units will cooperate closely with intelligence officers and facilitate in every way possible the expeditious accomplishment of the examination. Subject to modification to meet the particular situation, the prescribed system of evacuation for enemy personnel is shown in figure 1.

(3) Every effort will be made to expedite the transfer of prisoners from the front to the rear. The intelligence officer at each echelon, however, is responsible for deciding when an examination has been completed.

d. If the prisoners captured are so numerous that the examination of all is impracticable, only identifications and numbers will be noted and selected individuals briefly examined in the lower echelons. If practicable, officer prisoners will always be searched immediately after capture. The systematic search of enlisted prisoners will begin at the battalion collecting point if numbers permit, but in no case farther to the rear than the division collecting point.

e. In rapidly moving situations, there may be occasions when it will be impracticable for intelligence personnel of the lower echelons to make immediate examination of prisoners.

11. Action by unit effecting capture.—*a. Segregation of military personnel by classes.*—Immediately after capture, or as soon thereafter as possible, enemy officers, noncommissioned officers, and privates will be separated. They will be examined separately and kept in separate detachments or groups while on the way to the rear and in enclosures.

b. Disposition of effects.—Individuals or units effecting the capture of prisoners will permit them to retain steel helmets, gas masks, identification tags, insignia of rank, decorations, money, and objects of value. If time permits, all papers, maps, and documents of every kind will be appropriated and given to the guard for delivery with the prisoners at the regimental collecting point.

c. Procedure in front line units or units effecting capture.—

(1) *Enemy dead.*—Identifications will be determined and, if possible, all documents will be secured. Any remaining documents will be collected by the graves registration unit at the time of interment.

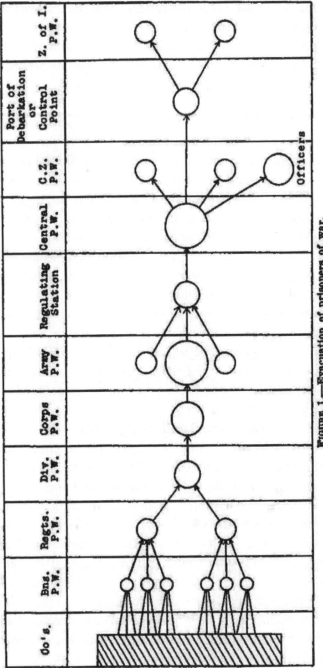

FIGURE 1.—Evacuation of prisoners of war.

(2) *Wounded prisoners.*—Identifications will be established from wounded prisoners and, if practicable, all documents found on them will be appropriated. If their physical condition permits, a brief examination may be made by intelligence officers to develop tactical information of immediate importance.

(3) *Unwounded prisoners.*—Unwounded prisoners will be disarmed immediately and rushed to the battalion collecting point where, if time permits, they will be searched and examined briefly for identification and information of immediate importance to the front line units; for example, items concerning the location of a machine gun, sniper post, or observation post. If the enemy speaks a different language, even this brief examination will generally be impracticable. *No attempt will be made to develop complete information.* Battalions will forward prisoners under guard to regimental collecting points and will telephone *immediately information concerning new identifications.* This information will be passed along the channels of command to theater headquarters.

12. Responsibility of guards.—Guards conducting prisoners to the rear will prevent them from talking and will deliver all captured documents placed in their care to higher headquarters. When it has been impracticable to search the prisoners prior to their evacuation, the guard will be directed to prevent the destruction of documents en route.

13. Procedure at regimental collecting points.—*a. During a period of stabilization.*—(1) In the vicinity of the regimental command post is the regimental collecting point where identifications will be checked and a brief examination conducted by the regimental intelligence officer, assisted by an enlisted interpreter, to develop tactical information of immediate importance to the regiment; for example, items concerning the organization and strength of the enemy's front line and any signs of impending attack or withdrawal. Prisoners should be questioned without unnecessary delay before they have had a chance to become composed and prepare their answers. It is at this stage of the examination that the examiner can bring fully into play his psychological sense and understanding of human nature, for at such a time the prisoners are at a distinct disadvantage.

(2) If the prisoners are numerous, the intelligence officer will question thoroughly only a few of the more intelligent who are likely to have information of value, such as observers, messengers, or liaison agents.

(3) The regimental intelligence officer will report to division headquarters the number of prisoners; the company, battalion, and regiment to which they belong; and the place and time of capture. The form shown in *b* below is suggested for this purpose.

(4) Tactical orders and maps found on the prisoners or turned over by the guard will be examined briefly for information on vital and immediate importance to the regiment. After this brief examination all documents pertaining to each prisoner should be tied together in one package, to which should be attached a resumé of his statements made during the examination. The following form is suggested:

Organization

INFORMATION FROM PRISONER OR DESERTER
(Line out one)

Place   Date   Hour

Last name   First name   Middle Initial   Serial No. | Résumé of statements

Grade   Company   Battalion   Regiment   Division

Where captured   Date and hour of capture

Signature

---

b. During a period of active operations.—(1) During a period of active operations the regimental intelligence officer will not have time to supervise all details relative to prisoners. Ordinarily it will be possible only to group the prisoners according to organization and then divide each group into three subgroups consisting of officers, noncommissioned officers, and privates, and list the number in each subgroup of each organization with place and time of capture. For this purpose the following form is suggested:

Organization							REPORT OF PRISONERS CAPTURED		
Place		Date		Hour					
Number of prisoners			Organization			Where captured	When captured	Important items of information	
Offi-cers	Non-com-mis-sioned officers	Privates	Com-pany	Bat-talion	Regi-ment				

Signature

(2) Time permitting, officers and noncommissioned officers will be searched and selected prisoners questioned briefly. In a rapidly moving situation, it will ordinarily not be possible to prepare individual cards giving a resumé of the examination as prescribed in *a* above.

14. Procedure at division collecting point.—*a.* At the division collecting point all prisoners will be searched or searched again, identifications checked, and additional tactical information developed, for example, items concerning the depth of the enemy organization and local reserves. The examination will not attempt to develop information which the division is not capable of fully exploiting at once. Appropriate tactical orders and maps found on prisoners or delivered by the guards should be inspected.

b. From the division the prisoners will be sent either to the corps or army prisoner of war enclosure, depending upon the plan of evacuation prescribed in administrative orders. In some situations they may even be sent to the central prisoner of war enclosure. The military police supervise the guarding and evacuation of prisoners from the division to the rear.

c. If prisoners are sent to the corps prisoner of war enclosure, the corps intelligence officer may conduct an additional tactical examination to develop information of particular importance to the corps; for example, items covering the entire depth of the hostile infantry and artillery positions. If they are not sent to the corps prisoner of war enclosure, the corps G-2 should send an examiner forward to division collecting points for the detailed information desired.

15. Procedure at army prisoner of war enclosure.—If the army is included in the system of evacuation, as it usually will be, it receives prisoners either direct from the division collecting points or from the corps prisoner of war enclosures. The army intelligence section should be prepared to conduct the final examination of all prisoners captured in the army area. Since in some situations prisoners may be sent direct to the central prisoner of war enclosure, the procedure and the scope of the final examination are given under the theater of operations.

16. Procedure at central prisoner of war enclosure in theater of operations.—*a. General.*—(1) The final examination will be conducted at the central prisoner of war enclosure by the intelligence section of theater headquarters. It may be delegated to the army and made at the army prisoner of war enclosure.

(2) Upon arrival at the central prisoner of war enclosure or army prisoner of war enclosure the prisoners will be assembled in an area set aside for the purpose. A military police officer assisted by an English-speaking noncommissioned officer prisoner or an interpreter of the intelligence service, will classify the prisoners by regiment, battalion, and company and then count them by units. At a designated hour each day he will render a report to the theater or army headquarters showing the number of prisoners, by organization and grade, received during the

previous 24-hour period. A copy of the report will be furnished G-2. The following form is suggested for the report:

Place

Date and hour

PRISONERS RECEIVED DURING THE PERIOD

-------------------------- to --------------------------

Number of prisoners			Organization		
Officers	Noncommissioned officers	Privates	Company	Battalion	Regiment

----
Signature

(3) During the sorting process an intelligence officer should make note of prisoners to be examined. He is interested in prisoners possessing information of the general organization of the enemy forces rather than those possessing tactical information. He should bear in mind that the private soldiers provide the greatest amount of information and the most truthful. Officers and noncommissioned officers who volunteer information should be distrusted. They generally give false information.

(4) After the sorting has been completed the prisoners should be conducted into the appropriate cages designated for those not yet examined. As they pass in, usually through a turnstile, an interpreter familiar with recruiting terms makes a record of each prisoner on the following form:

Place				RECORD OF PRISONERS RECEIVED DURING THE PERIOD				
Date and hour				----------------- to ------------------				
Last name	First name	Date of birth	Grade and organization	Date of induction	Number of draft	Civilian occupation	Wounds or diseases

Signature

(5) The officers should be examined as early as practicable after they are admitted to the cages and should be followed by the other prisoners selected by the intelligence officer at the time of sorting.

(6) The examination should be conducted as privately and secretly as possible in a special room set aside for the purpose. This will make it easier for the prisoner to talk without fear of denunciation or reprisal by his comrades. Only the examiner, his assistant, and the prisoner to be examined should be present.

(7) Prisoners who have been examined should be separated from those remaining to be examined. It is frequently desirable to place some of them in a room provided with a dictograph and containing a few intelligence agents.

b. Preparations for the examination.—In order that he may understand the personality, mentality, education, and civilian and military experience of a prisoner before the examination, the intelligence officer should study carefully all available data concerning the prisoner before he is brought into the examination room and should formulate a plan for the interrogation. This study should include an examination of the documents found on the prisoner, the reports of examinations at lower echelons of command, the statements made by the prisoner at the time he was turned in at the cage, and the history of his unit. Familiarity with conditions in the prisoner's organization enables the examiner to exploit fully the prisoner's pride, vanity, self-esteem, or pusillanimity. To develop additional information for use during the examination, it may also be desirable to place agents in the prisoner of war enclosure or cage for the purpose of gaining information to be used as a check on the accuracy of the statements of the prisoner and to assist the examining officer.

c. Conduct of examination.—(1) The examination should be carefully prepared. If given in a routine, perfunctory manner it will ordinarily accomplish nothing. It should have a definite purpose which is not simply making of record certain statements, but the determination of the enemy's projected operations or facts bearing upon the essential elements of information or upon conditions in the hostile army and country. The information desired may be revealed by some simple detail. The examiner should, therefore, have in mind the whole series of minor events which checked against each other may prove an hypothesis or suggest a procedure to be followed in making additional examinations.

(2) The examiner should be careful to maintain a military manner and attitude during the examination and should show evidence of character and energy. He should exact of the examined a correct and deferential attitude without resorting to severity.

(3) Certain prisoners remain silent or lie in their first answers, while others, encouraged by the complaisance of the examiner, give a flood of improvised information sometimes unconsciously suggested to them. Others, however, may be led progressively, by insidious questions and ingenious repetitions, to give unknowingly precisely the information desired. Sometimes the examiner must suggest the false in order to bring out the true. He should not repeat the examination conducted in the lower echelons but should confirm the main facts previously ascertained without going into the details.

(4) The examiner should have a tentative list of questions prepared, but should neither refer to it nor make notes during the interrogation. He should observe the methods of correct examination developed by

recognized law enforcement agencies where neither physical nor moral compulsion is employed. He should avoid useless discussions and judge from the first few words what is to be learned from the prisoner. Great care should be exercised in asking important questions. They should be inserted among routine questions, and the examiner should ask the important questions quite casually. It will frequently be advisable to ask several questions to which the answers are already known, inserting among these the important question to which the answer is not known. It is frequently advisable to make the prisoner believe that the official interrogation is over and to engage him in ordinary conversation, only to work back to the important question. There is nothing that gives more power or prestige to the examiner than to prove to a prisoner that he is not telling the truth. It will be found advantageous to act in such a way that the prisoner does not realize which question is the one to which a precise answer is desired; for example, by deliberately insisting upon certain points which are of no importance but which are made to appear important while posing the important question and making it appear of no particular importance and as having been asked only for good measure. All questions, regardless of their importance, should be precisely and accurately stated.

(5) It is frequently advisable for the examiner to assist the prisoner by making available to him a map, sketch, or aerial photograph from which he should be required to give an account of his movements. This procedure will assist him in recalling what he has seen and may also contribute to the final interpretation of an aerial photograph by clearing up details relative to enemy organization. It may even be desirable to take the prisoner to an observation post from which he can see the terrain and give precise information on points that need clarification.

(6) The examiner should conduct the examination in an objective manner. He should avoid rushing into a course of interrogation with a preconceived idea and attempt to make the prisoner say what he would like him to say. He should maintain an impartial and judicial attitude, without having in mind only the verification of a vague hypothesis. He should attempt to determine the truth. He must be sure of his grounds before resorting to suggestion, as that may lead the prisoner into saying unconsciously and in good faith what is

not true. On the other hand, the examiner must weigh and evaluate the accuracy of the prisoner's statements against the probabilities of error, misrepresentation, or hearsay. It is important to compare the statements of one prisoner with those of another and with information gathered from other sources. The examiner should also be on the alert and prepared to shift the course of the investigation if it takes an unexpected turn. He should not ask a prisoner for more than he can reasonably be expected to know.

(7) It is important to distinguish between what prisoners report they have seen and what they have heard. The statements of a prisoner are of greatest importance when he is talking of affairs or events in which he has participated. Many times, judging from facts already brought out in the examination, it may be determined that it would have been impossible for the prisoner to have seen or done the things he claims. Because of their greater familiarity with events, the statements of officers are of greater importance than those of enlisted men but are more likely to be false.

(8) Should enemy personnel having expert knowledge of artillery, tanks, communication, chemical, or aviation be available for examination, the examiner may request that an officer of the arm or service concerned be assigned to assist him.

d. *Questions for final examination.*—No list of questions can be prepared much in advance of the time of examination, as such a list will necessarily depend upon the information desired at the particular time. Theater headquarters will outline from time to time lists of questions for the final examination of personnel of the various arms and services. The questions actually used will vary with the information available to the person examined and the prisoner's mentality, willingness to tell the truth, and physical reaction to capture.

[. . .]

e. *Reports of examination.*—Immediate oral reports will be made by telephone to army or theater headquarters of any important change in previous reports or of any new developments. A complete written report in the form of a substantial resumé of information developed

A Japanese prisoner—a rare thing indeed—awaits questioning by a U.S. intelligence officer on the island of Guam, 1944. (NARA)

during the examination, together with the examiner's opinion as to its credibility, should follow. The written report, usually covering a period of 24 hours, is made in the evening and immediately dispatched to the G-2 office concerned.

17. Prisoners from enemy aviation and mechanization.—*a. Aviation personnel and parachute drops.*—Any military unit may become the collecting agency for enemy aviation personnel or personnel dropped by parachutes. The unit making the capture will at once post a guard over the airplane to prevent souvenir hunters and the curious from destroying it, collect all documents, report the capture through the nearest intelligence office to the army or theater headquarters by the most expeditious means of communication available, and send the prisoners and documents to the army or theater headquarters for examination.

b. Mechanized personnel.—Because of its great maneuverability and wide radius of action, an enemy mechanized force may strike deep into the territory under the control of our own forces. This is especially true in the early phases of operations. Proper defensive measures should result in the capture of personnel and equipment by either combat units or line of communication troops. In that event, report will be made to army or theater headquarters by the most expeditious means of communication available, and the prisoners and captured documents forwarded to the nearest intelligence officer for examination.

18. Enemy deserters.—*a. General.*—Deserters from enemy lines usually arrive during periods of quiet or just prior to an attack. They gladly volunteer information in the hope that they will receive better treatment than other prisoners of war. Escaped prisoners, if recaptured near the front, are likely to pose as deserters.

b. Treatment.—Enemy deserters will be examined in the various echelons of command in the same manner as other prisoners. They will be encouraged to talk and give their reasons for desertion.

c. Notation on report.—The enemy will do everything in his power to gain surprise. Accordingly, he may be expected to plant fake deserters bearing false documents. In making out reports of examination of deserters, intelligence officers will, therefore, note at the head of such a report "Information from deserter" in order that false information may be more easily checked and frustrated.

19. Enemy civilians.—During an advance in enemy territory, intelligence officers will examine enemy civilians for information regarding the enemy forces which occupied the evacuated area. Local officials and intelligent citizens, such as preachers or priests, teachers, postmasters, and stationmasters, will generally furnish the most reliable information.

[. . .]

SECTION IV
CAPTURED DOCUMENTS

22. Definition.—As used in this manual the term "document" includes maps; sketches, photographs; orders; tactical and technical manuals and instructions; code books; war diaries; newspapers; notebooks; service records; pay rolls; shoulder straps or other identifying marks on uniforms and individual equipment; post cards and letters; the records of headquarters, post and telegraph offices, telephone exchanges, banks, police stations, and municipal and government offices; and anything else of a similar class that may contain information relative to the hostile army or country.

23. Personal collections forbidden.—*The personal appropriation of documents is strictly forbidden. It is highly important that all documents be promptly turned into the proper unit commander or intelligence officer for as a whole they contain information of great importance to our forces.*

24. Object.—When systematically examined by trained personnel, captured documents constitute one of the principal sources of information available to a commander regarding the enemy order of battle, plans, morale, manpower, economic conditions, organization, armament, tactical and technical methods, methods of instruction, and many other subjects. All classes of documents will be examined at appropriate echelons of command with the object of developing therefrom all possible information of the enemy army and country. At the army and theater headquarters special offices and trained personnel will be provided for their examination.

25. Collecting agencies.—Documents are collected by reconnaissance detachments, front-line units, or other units effecting capture, from enemy dead, prisoners of war, and lately vacated enemy fortifications and installations; by graves registration units from enemy dead; by medical units from the enemy sick and wounded; by the censorship service from prisoners' mail; and by specially designated intelligence personnel from vacated enemy command post and business and governmental offices.

26. Classification.—*a. As to origin.*—Depending upon origin, documents may be classified as personal or official.

(1) Personal documents, such as post cards, letters, diaries, pay cards, and identifying marks are usually found on prisoners. The habit of preserving letters is so strong that, in any war with a civilized nation, they will always be a source of information in spite of the efforts of the enemy to break up the practice. Pay cards or service records captured in quantity make it possible to follow the whole process of recruitment, call to the colors, training, replacement, and hospitalization. Documents of this class are generally of little or no use in the lower echelons. They are of more importance to army and theater headquarters, for as a whole they tend to clarify the situation in the hostile army and country.

(2) Official documents are so varied in their nature that all units will find them useful sources of information. Corps and lower echelons should check official documents of a general nature, such as maps and operations and training orders, for information which can be immediately exploited. Among the most important official documents which may be captured are enemy codes, ciphers, and other cryptographic material. Work sheets used in the cryptographing of messages are of particular importance. Whenever an enemy message center or cryptographer is captured, special search should be made for codes, ciphers, and other cryptographic material.

b. As to military value.—Depending upon the nature of the information contained therein, documents may be classified as of immediate or general value.

(1) *Immediate value.*—Field orders, situation and operation maps, and documents giving projected operations or plans for the movement of important troop units are of immediate value. Information from documents of this kind should be transmitted to higher headquarters and affected adjacent units by the most expeditious means available.

(2) *General value.*—Tactical and technical manuals, war diaries, maps and aerial photographs, letters, newspapers, and other documents generally contain information which, though it cannot be immediately exploited, may assist in developing and keeping up-to-date the enemy order of battle or in clarifying the state of morale in the hostile army and country.

27. Transmission.—*a.* Documents captured by front line troops or reconnaissance detachments should be examined briefly for information of immediate importance to the regimental commander and then forwarded to the division G-2 by the guard conducting prisoners to the rear. Captured codes, ciphers, and cryptographic material will be transmitted to army or theater headquarters by the most rapid means of transportation available.

b. At the division collecting points, intelligence officers examine documents for additional information of immediate tactical importance. Time permitting, the documents found on each individual should be tied together in a package and tagged with a card inscribed "Information from prisoner or deserter," as prescribed in paragraph 13 *a.* The individual packages pertaining to the same company should be tied up and put in a sack. The company sacks of the same regiment should then be placed in a larger sack and marked with the number of the regiment and the place and date of capture. These precautions are necessary if the examiner at the army or central prisoner of war enclosure is to have a prisoner's papers before him during the final examination.

c. Documents found on wounded prisoners by medical units will be marked with the prisoner's name and organization and turned over to the unit intelligence officer for proper disposition.

d. Documents found by the graves registration units will be marked with the soldier's name, organization, and place where found and then turned over to the nearest intelligence officer for proper disposition.

e. After appropriate examination by the division, corps, and army echelons, all documents will be consolidated and forwarded to theater headquarters where trained intelligence personnel will subject them to final examination.

28. Final examination.—*a.* At theater headquarters, intelligence personnel qualified as translators of the enemy language will conduct the final examination. Proper organization of the work will expedite the examination. For this purpose all documents will be subjected to a brief preliminary examination and divided into three groups:

(1) Documents of immediate value.

(2) Documents of probable or general value.

(3) Documents of no value.

b. All documents of immediate value are then speedily and thoroughly examined and the information gleaned therefrom is prepared for transmittal to G-2. The documents are then suitably filed for future reference.

c. The documents of probable or general value are then examined and classified for file or destruction, depending upon their value. New tactical and technical regulations or instructions should be translated and forwarded to G-2 for transmittal to appropriate agencies for study.

d. Documents in code will be referred to the signal intelligence service.

e. All valueless documents will be destroyed.

Capture

The U.S. War Department was not only concerned about the information its intelligence services could extract from Axis prisoners of war. It was also focused on limiting the potential damage American POWs could inflict on the security of U.S. operations. An interesting counterpoint to the instructions concerning U.S. interrogation of the enemy is the War Department Pamphlet "If you should be CAPTURED these are your rights." The following are some key passages, drawing out the basic refrains of keeping silent and knowing your rights:

> Being a prisoner of war is a grim business.
>
> You live behind barbed wire, under constant guard.
>
> You are not going anywhere, because there is no rotation of prisoners of war. You are there for the duration. No furloughs, no leaves, not even a three day pass.
>
> The monotony is deadly.
>
> The whole thing is like an indeterminate sentence in the guardhouse. And the work details work harder and longer than the prisoners you used to watch when you were on prisoner guard back in the United States.
>
> But even the guardhouse prisoners back there were in a rich, friendly country. As a prisoner of war you are in enemy country, living with the enemy. You live no better than the enemy does, and hardly ever as well— never as well as a G.I. At best your captor is bound to treat you no better than he does his own soldiers stationed back in the rear. In Axis countries,

the pick of such food as they have goes to the front-line troops. Farther back, the population makes out with what is left. As a prisoner of war you won't get first call on that either.

Nevertheless, there are certain rules about being a prisoner of war. "The Geneva Convention Relative to the Treatment of Prisoners of War" contains rules which state what you must do and what you may not do. It also tells what the enemy may and may not do about you.

From the moment you are captured you have certain rights. Even before you are taken to a prisoner-of-war camp, these rights are in effect.

Stand up for your rights, but do it with military courtesy and firmness at all times. The enemy will respect you for it.

You must be humanely treated at all times.

Reprisals against you are not permitted. You cannot be punished for what somebody else has done.

You must be protected against insult or acts of violence by enemy military or civilians.

If you are wounded or sick, you are entitled to the same medical care as a member of the enemy's Army.

The enemy must clothe, feed, and shelter you.

You are a prisoner of war, not a criminal.

When you are questioned, by no matter what enemy authority, you must give only your name, rank, and serial number. Beyond that, there is no information which the enemy can legally force from you.

Do not discuss military matters of any sort with anyone.

An "Allied" soldier may be an enemy intelligence agent.

Forget all you ever knew about your own Army. If anyone wants to discuss it with you, even its insignificant details, say nothing.

You must surrender to the enemy who captured you all military equipment except your helmet and gas mask. However, the enemy must not take from you your personal belongings, such as your identification, insignia of rank, personal papers, wallet or photographs (unless of military value).

Money in your possession can be taken away from you only upon the order of an officer and after the amount has been determined. For this, you must be given a receipt. Demand a receipt. It is your right.

Any money taken from you must be entered to your account and returned to you when you are freed.

If you are an enlisted prisoner of war, you must salute all enemy officers. If you are an officer prisoner of war, you salute only enemy officers of equal or higher rank. You render your own salute, not the salute as executed by the enemy.

Where other matters of military courtesy and discipline are concerned, you have the same rights and duties as your opposite number in the enemy Army.

You are subject to all laws, regulations and orders enforced in the enemy army. You may be tried and if found guilty, punished for infractions of enemy regulations. However, no form of cruelty may be used in your punishment. Generally speaking, arrest, confinement and disciplinary punishment may be imposed upon you in the same manner as upon the enemy's own personnel of equivalent rank.

If you attempt to escape and are recaptured, you are liable only to disciplinary confinement not to exceed 30 days. But if you use violence, you may be punished for that violence quite apart from the 30 days imposed for the attempt to escape. If you commit any civilian crime, you become subject to punishments under enemy law and by enemy courts.

Having been punished for an attempted escape, that attempt may not be held against you if you try to escape again and are recaptured.

One of your most important rights is to request that a copy of the Geneva Convention Relative to the Treatment of Prisoners of War be shown to you. It should be in English.

If you do not ask for a copy of the Geneva Convention and read it, it is your own tough luck if certain of your rights are withheld from you.

All the rules of war under which you live as a prisoner are contained in the text of the Geneva Convention.

Don't let the formality of the title fool you. The text itself, which contains the information that is so important to you, is clearly and simply written. If, however, there are any points which are not clear to you, you have the right to ask the camp authorities, through your spokesman, for an explanation.

Let the Geneva Convention be your Basic Field Manual while you are in captivity.

Read it!

CHAPTER 3

Signals Intelligence, Cryptanalysis, and Cryptology

In its driest description, signals intelligence (SIGINT) can be defined as the targeting, detection, interception, and analysis of electronic signals from a foreign or hostile power for both tactical and strategic intelligence purposes. During World War II, the fortuitous alignment of several strands of technological development meant that SIGINT became the revolutionary branch of intelligence warfare in the conflict. SIGINT in itself is a blanket term, covering a spectrum of different technologies, processes, and strategic and tactical foci. Modern military thinking tends to include two sub-categories within SIGINT, these being COMINT, or communications intelligence, which refers to the interception of foreign communications between two parties, and ELINT, or electronic intelligence, denoting intelligence derived from the interception of non-communicative electronic signals, particularly radar. All of these elements came into play in World War II, with important results.

At a practical level during the conflict, the activities under the SIGINT banner broke down into four specific types. First, there was the interception of radio signals, the act of gaining access to the flow of enemy transmissions in the first place. Second came the business of traffic analysis (TA), in which the enemy communications were monitored and tracked to deduce significant patterns in the type, volume, content, and purpose of the transmissions. Third, there was the cryptanalysis of encoded or enciphered enemy communications, and fourth was the act of interpretation of the information extracted. To these categories we can add other elements, such as the design of secure codes and procedures for signals transmissions by friendly forces.

For the United States, SIGINT was both a strategic and a tactical effort. The following manual—Signal Corps Field Manual: Signal Corps Intelligence (1942)—acknowledges and explores both of these levels. The Signal Corps itself grew to be 350,000 personnel strong, and was one of the most powerful instruments in the SIGINT war, not only making major contributions to cryptanalysis and ELINT, but also to the development of U.S. cipher devices, radio countermeasures, and radar deception. It was also the parent organization for the Signal Intelligence Service (SIS) and the subsequent Signal Security Agency (SSA). In a new age of wireless warfare, the work of Signal Corps intelligence had battle-winning potential.

A U.S. Army Signal Corps soldier makes a field broadcast, relaying orders from the commanders around him. (U.S. Army Signal Corps)

★★★

From FM 11-35, *Signal Corps Field Manual: Signal Corps Intelligence* (1942)

CHAPTER 2
SIGNAL INTELLIGENCE SERVICE

Section I
GENERAL

■ 6. Duties.—The specific functions and duties of the Signal Intelligence Service may include any or all of the following:

a. Preparation, publication, storage, and distribution of codes and ciphers employed by our armed forces, and the repair and maintenance of cipher machines.

b. Interception of enemy radio and wire traffic by electrical means.

c. Location of enemy radio transmitting stations by radio position finding methods.

d. Solution of enemy codes and ciphers.

e. Development and preparation of secret inks to be employed by our own authorized agents and the detection of the presence of secret ink and other disguised writings in enemy documents.

f. Monitoring of friendly radio traffic in order to detect violations of signal security and the initiation of corrective measures.

■ 7. War Department.—The Signal Intelligence Service of the War Department is operated by the Chief Signal Officer to serve the military commander of the field force and his staff. The officer in charge of the Signal Intelligence Service is responsible for all of the duties outlined in paragraph 6. In addition to the personnel of the Signal Intelligence Service he has under his control such radio intelligence companies or detachments as may be required properly to perform his mission.

■ 8. THEATER OF OPERATIONS.—Organizations for the specific performances of signal intelligence activities may be allotted to expeditionary forces, defense commands, or task forces when the size of the force and the distances involved indicate the desirability of decentralizing signal intelligence activities. A portion of such organizations may be retained in a general reserve by the military commander of the field forces, for assignment as the situation dictates.

■ 9. ARMY.—A signal intelligence section is an integral part of the headquarters, signal service, army. The officer in charge of this section is responsible for the duties outlined in paragraph 4 which are within the capabilities and facilities of the section to perform. He has under his control the radio intelligence company assigned to the army.

■ 10. LOWER UNITS.—Signal Corps personnel within corps and divisions may be directed to assist in signal intelligence activities in addition to their signal communication duties. While signal intelligence is not a normal mission for signal communication personnel, all such personnel should be trained to recognize and immediately report any information of value to the signal intelligence effort. Examples of this type of information are violations of cryptographic security, heavy increases or silences in enemy radio transmission, description of captured or abandoned enemy signal communication or cryptographic equipment, intercepted enemy messages.

■ 11. RADIO INTELLIGENCE COMPANY.—The signal radio intelligence company is the basic information-gathering agency for signal intelligence. Through this unit the Signal Intelligence Service obtains the material for its study and evaluation.

■ 12. SPECIAL AGENCIES.—*a. Aircraft warning service.*—A highly specialized type of signal intelligence is furnished by the aircraft warning service. It is not a part of the Signal Intelligence Service of ground forces but a function under the direction of air force commanders. A detailed description of the aircraft warning service will be found in FM 11-25.

b. Censorship.—The Signal Corps is responsible for making the technical arrangements for the censorship of all electrical means of signal communication in the combat zone and in the communications zone if it is under martial law and to cover particular areas wherein censorship is established.

■ 13. ORGANIZATIONAL.—Table of Basic Allowances for Signal Corps prescribes certain equipment for issue to signal intelligence personnel and organizations. Radio intercept and direction-finding equipment is included therein. Secret and confidential cryptographic equipment issued by signal intelligence agencies to tactical organizations is not listed in Tables of Basic Allowances.

■ 14. SPECIAL EQUIPMENT.—Much of the equipment used by signal intelligence agencies is highly technical and secret. No authorized allowances of such equipment are prescribed.
It is provided as needed and may include the following:
a. Tabulating machines for use in code compilation and in cryptanalysis.
b. Laboratory equipment and supplies for secret ink preparation and detection.
c. Equipment and supplies for cryptanalytic research and the development of new cipher devices.
d. Reproducing equipment and supplies necessary for the packing and shipping of codes, cipher machines, and cipher keys.
e. A library consisting of various technical books, dictionaries, periodicals. and other sources of general information.
f. Tools and supplies for the repair and maintenance of cipher machines.

SECTION II
WAR DEPARTMENT

■ 15. GENERAL.—The Signal Intelligence Service, War Department, operates under the direction of the Chief Signal Officer. It has under its control a varying number of radio intelligence companies (T/O 11-77) and fixed station radio intercept detachments. The signal radio intelligence companies and fixed station detachments constitute a field force which gathers information over wide areas and places it at the disposal of the Signal Intelligence Service. The latter can be considered as a centralized laboratory which analyzes the material received and as rapidly as possible furnishes to the chief of staff, field forces, the concrete information obtained.

■ 16. DETAILED ORGANIZATION.—*a.* The Signal Intelligence Service is, in general, organized into sections as follows:

    Administrative section.
    Radio intelligence section.
    Security section.
    Laboratory section.
    Code and cipher compilation section.
    Code and cipher solution section.

b. A description of the organization of a signal radio intelligence company will be found in FM 11-20 [see below].

c. Certain additional organizations may be assigned to the Signal Intelligence Service for such purposes as interruption of wire lines, wire tapping, and photographic missions. The composition, size, and equipment of these detachments will depend upon the particular circumstances of their employment.

■ 17. OFFICER IN CHARGE.—The officer in charge of the War Department Signal Intelligence Service is an assistant to the Chief Signal Officer. He is responsible to the Chief Signal Officer for the operation of the Signal Intelligence Service including assigned and attached radio intelligence companies. In the name of the Chief Signal Officer he issues such orders and directives as may be necessary to the radio intelligence companies and other organizations which may be assigned for signal intelligence duties. He has direct supervision over all activities of the Signal Intelligence Service. He maintains liaison with such members of the G-2 section of the War Department General Staff as are concerned with the functions of signal intelligence, and with the approval of the Chief Signal Officer, is the technical adviser to G-2 on such matters.

■ 18. ADMINISTRATIVE SECTION.—The Administrative section is responsible for the administration and supply of the Signal Intelligence Service. The officer in charge of this section assists the officer in charge of the Signal Intelligence Service in the supervision of all activities and in securing prompt and effective operation. The section is responsible for all correspondence between the Signal Intelligence Service and other offices or organizations. The securing of special technical equipment not provided through normal supply channels is a responsibility of this section.

■ 19. RADIO INTELLIGENCE SECTION.—This section is responsible for the technical supervision of the War Department radio intelligence companies. It carries out this responsibility by performing the following duties:

a. Preparation of plans for the interception of radio traffic and location of enemy transmitters to include directives to be given the radio intelligence companies. [. . .]

b. By agreement with the security section, the preparation of plans and directives to the radio intelligence companies for the monitoring of friendly traffic.

c. Submission to the code and cipher solution section of intercepted enemy traffic and cooperation with that section to insure that cryptographed messages in the quantity and type needed to facilitate solution are made available.

d. Evaluation of information received from the position-finding activities of the radio intelligence companies to include probable location of stations, call signs, frequencies, net grouping, and any peculiar operating characteristics.

e. Submission of daily reports to G-2 on volume of traffic, movement of stations, and radio silences, to assist him in evaluating all information and in determining the enemy's capabilities.

f. Submission to the security section of reports on violations of signal security obtained by monitors.

g. Preparation of plans for the coordination of the activities of radio intelligence companies assigned to armies and subordinate commands in order that duplication may be avoided and that the position-finding and intercept units of all the field forces may function as a team.

■ 20. SECURITY SECTION.—The security section has the primary mission of detecting and preventing violations of signal security. It has a secondary mission of planning for wire interruption and wire tapping. It carries out its missions by performing the following duties:

a. Preparation of plans in collaboration with the radio intelligence section for the monitoring of friendly radio traffic.

b. Study of reports furnished by the radio intelligence section on instances of signal security violation including violations of cryptographic security to determine the extent of damage done.

c. Preparation of corrective orders and disciplinary measures aimed at preventing violations of security.

d. Advising the code compilation section when cryptographic systems have been compromised in order that replacements may be issued and the compromised systems rescinded.

e. Preparation of plans and directives for the employment of dummy radio stations, sending of false messages, and other methods of radio deception.

f. Preparation of plans and directives for the use of wire tapping and wire interrupting detachments.

g. Provision of proper safeguards to prevent the enemy from tapping or interrupting friendly wire lines.

■ 21. LABORATORY SECTION.—The laboratory section operates a secret ink laboratory. It is charged with both the development and detection of secret inks and cryptic methods other than code or cipher. It performs as required the following duties for G-2:

a. Preparation and issue of secret inks for use by intelligence agents.

b. Examination of documents suspected of containing secret ink, microphotography, or other espionage methods of writing.

c. Examination of mail of suspected enemy agents where the fact of such examination is desired to be kept unknown.

d. Preparation of photostatic or photographic copies of evidence against espionage agents which have been obtained by the secret inks laboratory.

■ 22. Code and Cipher Compilation Section.—The responsibilities of this section include the following:

a. Compilation, production, and distribution of codes and ciphers in use by the field forces.

b. Issue and maintenance of cipher machines.

c. Preparation and issue of instructions covering the employment of cryptographic systems.

d. Periodic issue of cipher keys for systems used in signal communication.

e. Provision of secure storage for reserve cryptographic equipment.

f. Notification to all agencies concerned of the effective date of changes in cryptographic systems.

g. Destruction of superseded cryptographic equipment.

■ 23. Code and Cipher Solution Section.—The code and cipher solution section will be organized into a number of sub-sections depending upon the number and type of enemy cryptographic systems under study. In general its duties are:

a. Analysis of intercepted enemy messages in code and cipher for the purpose of solving enemy systems.

b. Translation of messages in systems which can be solved.

c. Indexing and filing of all intercepted enemy traffic.

d. Preparation in cooperation with the radio intelligence section of plans for the interception of the particular type of encrypted traffic desired.

e. Submission to G-2 of the translations of solved messages.

f. Furnishing to the signal intelligence services of armies and any other subordinate commands all available material to permit local translation of intercepted messages.

g. Preparation of technical reports on new cryptanalytic methods for instructional and historical purposes.

h. Technical coordination of the solution activities in all subordinate signal intelligence companies.

i. Design and development of equipment for cryptanalytic employment

Section III
ARMY

■ 24. General.—The Signal Intelligence Service assigned to an army consists of the signal intelligence section of the headquarters, signal service, army (T/O 11-200-1) plus one or more radio intelligence companies (T/O 11-77). Special wire detachments for tapping or interrupting wire lines may be provided from time to time. The signal intelligence section is strictly an operating agency. It is not organized to perform any of the research or production duties of the Signal Intelligence Service of the War Department.

■ 25. Detailed Organization.—The signal intelligence section being much smaller and having more limited duties than the corresponding service of the War Department, no definite suborganization is prescribed. Subsections will be set up corresponding to the duties performed and the following four subsections would normally be found:

Administrative.

Radio intelligence.

Security.

Solution.

■ 26. Officer in Charge.—The officer in charge of the army signal intelligence section is an assistant to the army signal officer. He is responsible to the army signal officer for the supervision and conduct of signal intelligence activities within the army. In the name of the army signal officer he issues orders and directives to the one or more radio intelligence companies assigned to the army. With the approval of the army signal officer he maintains close contact with the G-2 section of the Army general staff and acts as technical adviser to G-2 on signal intelligence matters. He exercises direct control over the signal intelligence section. He cooperates with the Signal Intelligence Service of the War Department under whose technical supervision he functions to attain the necessary coordination of all signal intelligence agencies of the field forces.

■ 27. ADMINISTRATIVE SUBSECTION.—The administrative sub-section is responsible for the supply and administration of the signal intelligence section. The officer in charge of this sub-section assists in the general supervision of all army signal intelligence duties. The handling of all correspondence between the signal intelligence section and other offices or organizations is a responsibility of this subsection.

■ 28. RADIO INTELLIGENCE SUBSECTION.—The radio intelligence subsection exercises technical supervision over the one or more radio intelligence companies assigned to the army. It is responsible for the following duties:

a. Preparation of plans for the interception of enemy radio traffic and location of enemy transmitters, to include directives to be given the radio intelligence companies.

b. By agreement with the security subsection, the preparation of plans and directives to the radio intelligence companies for the monitoring of friendly traffic.

c. Submission to the solution subsection of intercepted enemy traffic which can be translated without lengthy cryptanalytic study.

d. Submission to the administrative subsection of intercepted enemy traffic which cannot be translated for forwarding to the Signal Intelligence Service of the War Department.

e. Evaluation of information received from the position-finding activities of the radio intelligence companies to include probable location of stations, call signs, frequencies, net grouping, and any peculiar operating characteristics.

f. Submission of daily reports to G-2 based on volume of traffic, movement of stations, and radio silences, to assist him in evaluating all information, and in determining the enemy's capabilities.

g. Submission to the security subsection of reports on violations of signal security obtained by monitors.

■ 29. SECURITY SUBSECTION.—The security subsection is responsible for the following duties:

a. Study of reports furnished by the radio intelligence sub-section on instances of signal security violations, including violations of cryptographic security, to determine the extent of damage.

b. Preparation of corrective orders and disciplinary measures aimed at preventing violations of signal security.

c. Informing the Signal, Intelligence Service, War Department, of compromised cryptographic systems.

d. Preparation of plans and directives for the employment of dummy radio stations, the sending of false messages, and methods of radio deception as directed by G-2.

e. Preparation of plans and directives for the use of wire tapping and wire interrupting detachments and the initiation of action to obtain such detachments.

f. Provision of proper safeguards to prevent the enemy from tapping or interrupting friendly wire lines.

g. Receipt from the Chief Signal Officer and distribution within the Army of such cryptographic equipment and replacements as may be issued from time to time.

■ 30. SOLUTION SUBSECTION.—This subsection, unlike the code and cipher solution section, Signal Intelligence Service, War Department, does not perform original cryptanalysis. It is dependent upon the latter for material enabling the decryptographing of enemy traffic. Its primary duties are:

a. Decryptographing and translating of enemy messages in systems for which the solution has been furnished by the War Department.

b. Arranging with the radio intelligence subsection for the maximum interception of traffic in known systems.

c. Submission to G-2 of the translations of messages.

d. Maintenance of close contact with the Signal Intelligence Service of the War Department on all matters affecting solution activities.

CHAPTER 3
SIGNAL INTELLIGENCE SERVICE PROCEDURE

SECTION I
RADIO INTELLIGENCE

■ 31. GENERAL.—Radio intelligence is the most prolific source of signal intelligence information. It is of two forms: radio intercept and radio position finding. The radio intelligence companies have been organized for the sole purpose of securing this type of information. Radio intelligence companies are assigned as an organic part of each army. They may also be assigned to defense commands, task forces, or other special missions. They are sometimes employed independently for frontier or coast defense or for counterintelligence in the zone of the interior. It should be noted that their disposition is based on technical and not tactical decisions. The primary consideration governing all radio intelligence operations is that information be placed at the disposal of commanders in sufficient time for effective countermeasures

■ 32. COMPANY.—The organization, duties, and operating methods of the radio intelligence company are discussed in detail in FM 11-20 [see below].

■ 33. RADIO INTERCEPT.—Radio intercept is made of messages in the clear and messages in code or cipher. Clear text messages are normally only of immediate action value and individually of minor importance; taken in volume they frequently give an indication of enemy dispositions and probable lines of action. The decision as to value, however, should not be made by the intercepting operator but by the officer responsible for the intercept directive. If the directive calls for guarding a certain frequency or channel, all traffic heard should be copied and submitted. If the directive asks for specific types of traffic, only those types need be copied, although any traffic heard which is of known value should be copied whether covered by directive or not. When speed of transmission, volume of traffic, or weak signals render direct copying difficult, transmissions are recorded on equipment provided for the purpose and transcribed by the intercepting agency at the earliest opportunity. All intercept is of value only if it is handled speedily. Intercepted traffic normally is sent by messenger from the intercepting agency to the Signal Intelligence Service under which it operates. Frequent scheduled messenger service must be established. Telephone or telegraph should be used to supplement the messenger service, particularly in cases requiring urgent action. The use of radio to forward intercepted traffic is inadvisable.

■ 34. RADIO POSITION FINDING.—Radio position finding is dependent upon close cooperation between radio intercept stations and radio direction-finding stations. The radio intelligence company functions as a team composed of direction-finding stations and intercept stations. The intercept stations locate enemy signals by searching a limited portion of the radio spectrum or by guarding certain channels. A located signal is reported by telephone to the direction-finding stations and simultaneous bearings are taken. The determination of probable position is accomplished by plotters assigned to the control section. Radio direction finding is based on the two facts that radio waves travel in great circular paths, and that a properly constructed rotatable receiving antenna will give minimum response when its plane is at right angles to the direction of the radio wave. In taking bearings two sources of error are present: first, the inability of the operator to locate the exact point of minimum response; second, the fact that radio waves are affected by the presence of electrical conductors, terrestrial irregularities, so-called "magnetic storms," and other factors which cause refractions in the great circle paths. Careful analysis based on locally obtained data will assist in reducing this second type of error, but it must always be assumed to be present and to increase with the radio frequency of the signal. Consequently, highly accurate results in position finding cannot be expected. It is generally safe to assume that each bearing is accurate to within 10°. The probable location is determined from the plotting of three or more azimuths.

■ 35. SIGNAL SECURITY MISSIONS.—Signal security missions are frequently assigned to the intercept sections of the radio intelligence company.

These missions consist of the monitoring of friendly radio stations in accordance with directives furnished by the Signal Intelligence Service. In monitoring a friendly station or net all transmissions are copied but normally only those about which there is a question as to signal security violation are forwarded to the Signal Intelligence Service. The usual violations of signal security are—

a. Unauthorized or unwarranted transmission of radio messages in the clear.

b. Improper use of cryptographic systems.

c. Violation of radio silence.

Section II
SIGNAL SECURITY

■ 36. CRYPTOGRAPHIC.—Codes and ciphers, unless properly used, cannot be expected to provide security against enemy intelligence. AR 380-5 sets forth the basic rules governing the use of cryptographic systems. In addition, each code or cipher system is generally accompanied by instructions which apply specifically to that system. No person should attempt the use of any cryptographic system unless and until he is thoroughly familiar with both the general and specific instructions. The life of any code must be considered fairly short, since there are many opportunities for physical compromise. Cipher systems are designed so that their crypto-graphic security lies in a changeable key and the system may remain in effect, after compromise, by simply changing the key. Cipher systems, while offering greater flexibility, are generally more vulnerable to hostile cryptanalysis. Enciphered code will provide the greatest security, but it is usually too slow for field use. It is the duty of the Signal Intelligence Service to provide suitable cryptographic systems, to insure their proper use by instruction and by monitoring, and to effect immediately the replacement of systems which have been compromised.

■ 37. RADIO.—The radio transmitter is the most prolific source of intelligence in field operations. Radio transmission in the clear is justified only in situations when the time available to the enemy is insufficient for exploitation of the information contained in the message. Under no circumstances should personal convenience affect the decision to send in clear. Time is the only consideration. Radio should be considered as an auxiliary means of communication supplementing wire and messenger service. Under many conditions radio is the only possible means but if choice exists wire or messenger is to be preferred. Radio security consists not only of guarding what is transmitted, but of limiting the use of radio to actual necessity. Enemy intelligence may be served by every transmission from a friendly station. Even though the message may be unintelligible, every transmission must be assumed to disclose the identity of both transmitting and receiving stations, and the location of the transmitting station (and of the receiving station also if the message is acknowledged). It is for this reason that radio silence is frequently ordered prior to the actual commencement of offensive operations. To enforce radio security the Signal Intelligence Service is responsible for the monitoring of friendly radio transmissions and the initiation of corrective or disciplinary measures where necessary.

■ 38. WIRE.—While immeasurably safer than radio, wire communication is not completely reliable from the security viewpoint. It is not secure against enemy espionage agents. With some types of wire lines physical tapping may not be necessary, for interception can be accomplished by electric induction. This is particularly true of ground return circuits. Interception by induction, however, requires the presence in the vicinity of the wire line of detecting and amplifying equipment. By the enforcement of proper measures, wire communication can be accorded a fairly high degree of security. These measures consist of—

a. *Policing wire lines by electric means.*—By the use of test sets the attempt at wire tapping on any line frequently can be detected. When an unauthorized telephone is cut in on a line the electric characteristics of the line are slightly changed. This change may be detected on the meter of a test set.

b. *Surveillance on the part of operators.*—All operators should be trained to challenge any suspicious voice or sound indicating the presence on the line of unauthorized listeners. The circumstances should be immediately reported to the wire chief for investigation.

c. Use of armed guards.—Armed guards should be detailed to police the length of any wire lines believed to be in danger of interception. It is the only offense against interception by induction, which cannot be detected by electric means.

d. Training of using personnel.—Regardless of the safeguards employed, no wire line of normal length can be considered as perfectly secure. All personnel must be cautioned against discussing on the telephone any information of vital importance. All secret messages should be crytographed before transmitting by telegraph.

■ 39. AUTHENTICATION.—One of the most important and effective of all security measures is the use of authentication, which has a twofold purpose. It assures the recipient of a message that the transmitting agent is bona fide; conversely, it assures the transmitting agent that the recipient is bona fide, which is equally important. To be effective, authentication should be applied to each message rather than periodically between transmitting and receiving agencies. Too much dependence should not be placed on recognizing voices. The fidelity of radio voice transmission is frequently poor and the sound of a familiar voice can be imitated by enemy agents. Few personal characteristics are inherent in telegraphic transmissions either by radio or wire, and without some means of authentication the recognition of transmissions as bona fide is impossible. It is a responsibility of the Signal Intelligence Service to provide suitable authentication systems when required. The authenticator group is transmitted in the heading of the message or, in the case of voice transmission, immediately after contact has been established. An insecure authentication system which the enemy may solve and use is worse than none at all, for it causes reliance to be placed on a false message which might otherwise have been questioned. Authentication systems possessing the desired degree of security fall generally in one of the following two classes:

a. Prearranged lists.—A list of words, letters, or numerals is prepared and furnished all correspondents. The words, letters, or numerals are then used in regular order, one at a time, to authenticate each message. When once used, the authenticator is crossed off the list and not used again. This method is particularly effective between two correspondents. As the number of correspondents increases it becomes more difficult for any one correspondent to select the next authenticator on the common list. In such cases the correspondent attempting to establish his identity can be given the last used authenticator and told to supply the following one.

b. Additive method.—A more flexible method applicable to a large number of correspondents is that involving the principle of addition. According to a key furnished all correspondents, a numerical cipher is substituted for the letters of the alphabet and is employed as indicated below. Assume the following numerical cipher to be in effect:

A	B	C	D	E	F	G	H	I	J	K	L	M	N	O	P	Q	R	S	T	U	V	W	X	Y	Z
4	8	5	6	2	0	1	3	7	9	0	5	2	4	3	8	1	0	7	2	6	3	9	4	9	2

The receiving operator challenges the transmitting operator by asking him to authenticate any three letters at random, for example, KRP. The transmitting operator adds the numerical equivalents of these letters and replies "8." He may then challenge the receiving operator to ascertain that the person or station answering is the intended receiver of the message, for example, asking him to authenticate BXS. When the reply "19" is given, authentication has been established between both parties.

Section III
SECRET INK LABORATORY

■ 40. PREPARATION OF SECRET INKS.—A secret ink laboratory operates under the signal intelligence division, War Department, and theater of operations. The officer in charge of the laboratory section directs the activities of the secret ink laboratory. One of the duties with which the laboratory is charged is the preparation of secret inks for the use of such Intelligence agents as may be authorized by the Assistant Chief of Staff, G–2. The laboratory instructs these agents in the use of the ink, furnishes them with a supply for their mission, develops communications received from such agents, and prepares communications addressed to them. The composition of secret inks and the manner of their use and development is secret information and cannot be covered in this manual.

■ 41. DETECTION OF SECRET INKS.—A more continuous activity of the laboratory is the examination of suspected documents for the presence of secret ink. In some cases the fact of such examination is purposely concealed from the addressee of the document. In others the secret writing must be photographed to provide permanent evidence of its existence. This is frequently a difficult operation, due to the dimness or very [illegible] period of legibility of the writing. The secret ink laboratory assists in censorship work in the theater of operations by examining suspected documents. It assists in setting up facilities for secret ink detection in such locations as may be directed by the officer in charge of censorship and provides technical supervision over such examining stations. The methods used in secret ink detection are covered in secret documents prepared by the Chief Signal Officer.

■ 42. OTHER ACTIVITIES.—In addition to secret inks there are many other methods of transmitting information, the detection of which requires laboratory analysis. Among the more common of such methods are—

a. Microscopic writing.—This can performed only by a highly skilled person. By using a pen or some other instrument, minute writing is inscribed on a hair, a grain of rice, or other appropriate object. Engraving may be applied glass or a similar hard polished substance. Such methods, while, frequently undetectable to the naked eye, may discovered by microscopic examination.

b. Microphotography.—A highly successful method requiring no artistic skill employs microphotography. By this method a letter-size piece of paper is photographed on specially prepared film and reduced to small dimensions.

c. Invisible photographs.—A photographic print can be rendered invisible by applying a certain chemical solution. In transit the print appears as a blank piece of paper or may contain visible writing to avoid suspicion. The recipient is able to restore the original print by applying to it the proper chemical solution.

d. Writing under stamps.—A common method is that of writing in small script and pasting a postage stamp over the writing, This method may be detected in a number of ways.

SECTION IV
CODE AND CIPHER COMPILATION

■ 43. CODE COMPILATION.—Codes are of two kinds. A *one-part* code is a list of code groups and corresponding meanings both arranged in alphabetical order. A *two-part* code consists of two lists; in the first or encoding section the meanings are arranged alphabetically and the corresponding code groups are assigned in random order; in the decoding section the code groups are arranged alphabetically and opposite each appears its meaning. The compilation of a two-part code is more of a task but such a code possesses far greater cryptographic security. Code groups are selected from a permutation table which is prepared for each code and shows the possible combinations of letters. It provides for sufficient dissimilarity between groups to avoid erroneous meanings, resulting from telegraphic errors. A revision of a one-part code cannot be made without changing the permutation table. Successive editions of a two–part code may be compiled with the same permutation table by simply shutting the groups. The use of tabulating machinery is indispensable in code compilation. The Signal Intelligence Service has full technical responsibility for code compilation; it shares a joint responsibility with the using arms and services for the selection of adequate and concise plain text meanings. The using arms and services should make recommendations whenever necessary for the addition or deletion of meanings.

■ 44. CIPHER SYSTEMS AND KEYS.—Cipher systems fall into two general classes. In a *substitution cipher* the letters of the plain text are replaced by cipher equivalents as determined by a key. In a *transposition cipher* the letters of the plain text are retained but their relative position is changed in accordance with a key. The key is an element of variable nature which controls or directs encipherment and decipherment. It frequently consists of an easily remembered word, phrase, or group of numbers. A combination of the two methods is sometimes employed. The preparation of a cipher consists therefore of two elements: a description of the method to be employed and a list of keys. When a code becomes compromised the issue of a new code book becomes necessary, whereas the compromise of a cipher in general compromises only a particular key. Because of their simplicity in handling, cipher keys are changed frequently. No cipher system should be issued without at least one emergency key which can be put into effect upon notification. Cipher systems may be applied to encoded messages to increase security. This practice is normally followed when compromise of the code book is suspected and immediate replacement of the code is not possible.

■ 45. USE OF TABULATING EQUIPMENT.—The preparation of codes and certain types of cipher keys is greatly facilitated and much time is saved by the use of tabulating machines. The operation of these machines requires the services officer and enlisted personnel who have had experience with tabulating equipment. The method of using the tabulating machines is beyond the scope of this manual.

■ 46. CIPHER MACHINES.—In addition to the manually employed cipher methods mentioned in paragraph 44, cipher devices or machines are used for the purpose of increasing both security and speed. Some of these devices are of rather complicated construction and present the same problem of maintenance as radio apparatus. Since these devices are secret or confidential, they are not handled through normal supply channels. The Signal Intelligence Service is responsible for the issue and replacement of this equipment. Trained personnel to make repairs, a shop with necessary tools and equipment, and a supply of spare parts for replacement are included in the Signal Intelligence Service, War Department, and theater of operations.

SECTION V
CRYPTANALYSIS

■ 47. GENERAL.—Cryptanalysis is an analytical science. A successful code and cipher solution section requires personnel trained in this science. Much of the work is clerical in nature, however, and a successful solution section may be built around a few expert cryptanalysts assisted by an adequate force of competent clerks. The translation of messages in systems which have been solved is expedited by the use of labor-saving devices and other special equipment. The use of equipment as well as many of the cryptanalytic procedures is secret information and is contained in secret technical manuals.

■ 48. BASIC OPERATIONS.—Four basic operations govern all cryptanalytic procedure. They are—

a. Determination of language.—Normally this presents no great problem in field operations as it may be assumed to be the mother tongue of the enemy. In the case of messages intercepted from espionage agents the determination may not be so simple. Indications of a particular language may be found in the heading or signature and in the absence of certain letters or the addition of accented letters. If the language cannot be determined, cryptanalysis proceeds and the language is determined later.

b. Determination of general system.—This is by far the most difficult phase of cryptanalysis and success cannot be attained without a determination of the general system employed. It requires an exhaustive study of available text with the elimination, one by one, of cryptographic methods of known characteristics which do not apply. Errors on the part of enemy code clerks are most helpful in this determination. Information gathered from other intelligence agencies may also be of great value. Once the system has been determined, a definite plan of attack can be made and cryptanalysis may then proceed along intelligent lines with a definite objective in view.

c. Reconstruction of specific key.—Cryptographic systems other than straight code depend for their security upon a specific and changeable key which will still afford protection when the basic system has been discovered. The reconstruction of the key or keys used in messages under study must therefore precede or advance concurrently with the reconstruction of plain text. Generally the reconstruction of one key will assist in the reconstruction of others, and a cryptographic system cannot be considered as solved unless messages can be read in at least a majority of the keys used.

d. Reconstruction of plain text.—In this step the assistance of a qualified linguist in the language used is essential, for frequently assumptions of words must be made. Correct assumptions can be proved when tested against the general system and the proved or assumed specific key. When completely reconstructed and proved, the plain text is translated into English if the original message was in a foreign language.

■ 49. RESULTS.—*a. Time.*—It must be remembered that successful cryptanalysis cannot be given a time limit. Solution depends to a large extent on intelligent recognition and application of information supplied through the errors of enemy code clerks. Ultimate solution of cryptographic systems cannot be expected in all cases. Success is normally attainable only as a result of long and patient study aided by such "breaks" as the enemy may afford through misuse of his cryptographic systems.

b. Accuracy.—The accuracy of results attained by the solution of enemy messages should be emphasized. Successful application of cryptanalytic principles in effecting solution provides results whose accuracy cannot be doubted. In other words, cryptoanalysis produces results which are entirely correct or it produces no result at all. The procedure is based upon the absolute check of each assumption made and consequently the final result is a product of cross-checked elements. The highest reliability can be placed on information obtained through the solution of cryptographed enemy messages.

★★★

The deployment of intelligence units in tactical contexts is a focus of the Signal Corps' 1940 manual Organization and Operations in Corps, Army Theater of Operations, and GHQ. *At the beginning of the war, the chief types of tactical SIGINT units were radio intelligence platoons within divisional signal companies and signal radio intelligence (SRI) companies assisting field armies. Notably, these companies did not have organic analysis personnel within their structure; the information they derived was instead passed up to analysts within the theater staff. The arrangement was fine for peacetime, but wartime conditions revealed its inadequacies, being slow to process information and offering limited support to the corps level of command. Thus in 1942–43 the tactical signals elements of Army formations in the MTO and ETO were progressively revised, with measures such as establishing two radio signal platoons within the corps signal battalion and developing corps signal service companies that included their own analytical teams. From 1944 and particularly by the time of the D-Day landings, specialist signals units were sown widely throughout the Army's major frontline operational structures, with greater flexibility of response to operational needs.*

Radio transmissions

U.S. military analysis of Axis communications was not just useful for gaining insight into enemy tactics, intentions and procedures. It could also provide a mirror in which the efficiency and security of Allied signals communications could be studied. The following is from the pages of the Intelligence Bulletin *in November 1942:*

A captured Italian Intelligence Report states that in communications during field operations the British have made "abundant use of abbreviations, conventional words, names, and agreed phrases." The Italians admit that these methods have proved effective. "In particular," the report says, "key words for deciphering messages giving fresh positions have been well thought out. It has been observed that, by way of a change from past practice, two different codes have been used in a single message, one code in numbers and the other in words. For example, 'Position of Pura is Jsy. A5N.' Such messages take our cipher expert so long to unravel that the information they contain is useless to us."

This is good news—for our side. Nevertheless, from the same source the American soldier can pick up a few tips about how *not* to send radio messages in the field. The British used to rely heavily on frequent changes of names, frequencies, and key words or numbers. Instead of confusing Axis listeners, this kind of thing tended to make them more alert. The British soon learned that instead of changing codes frequently, it was better to change them cleverly. For example, certain units, whose code names had been changed had been including references to earlier messages transmitted under their former names; these references specifically mentioned the old names and dates. In these cases identification of the unit by the Axis was a simple matter. Also, apparently unimportant messages helped in identifying certain infantry battalions about which the Axis had very little information.

It is interesting and useful to know what communication methods make field operations easier for the enemy and what methods make them more difficult. The captured Italian report reveals that the British often have puzzled the enemy by using cockeyed slang and double-talk. It must be stressed, however, that this method does not guarantee safety. For example, the American expression "Keep your shirt on" might mean nothing to the enemy, but on the other hand it might mean a great deal—because the Axis armies include many men who have lived in the United States.

$\star\star\star$

From FM 11-20, *Signal Corps Field Manual: Organization and Operations in Corps, Army Theater of Operations, and GHQ* (1940)

Section V
RADIO INTELLIGENCE COMPANY

[. . .]

■ 70. OPERATING PLATOON.—*a. General.*—The operating platoon comprises a position finding section, an intercept section, and a control section. Operations of each of these sections are interrelated and the entire platoon operates as a team. The intercept section performs searching and guarding operations. (See *b* below.) The control section, observing the immediate results of such operations, assigns targets to direction finding stations. Data obtained by the direction finding stations are transmitted to the control section where they are utilized to determine the position of the designated target. The control section, through its platoon commander, transmits information obtained to higher headquarters. The organization of each section into teams is shown in figure 17.

b. Intercept section.—The intercept section consists of the section chief and two reliefs of four radio operators each. It is capable of 24-hour operation of four radio intercept receivers. The intercept section operates at the location of the control section and provides the latter section with the information required for directing the operations of the position finding section. Transportation allotted to the section will permit operations of the section to be conducted in the vehicles in which it is transported. Missions are assigned to the section by the platoon commander or, in his absence, by the chief of the control section. The section is assigned both searching and guarding missions.

(1) Searching missions include rapidly searching the radio frequency spectrum for signals of enemy and friendly stations and reporting to the

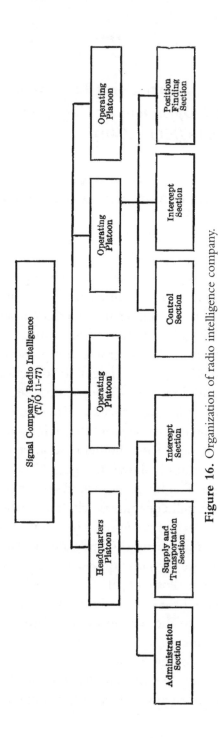

Figure 16. Organization of radio intelligence company.

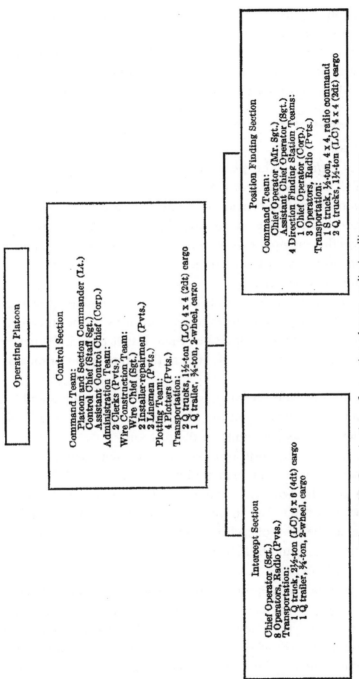

Figure 17. Organization of operating platoon, radio intelligence company.

control sections results obtained. These reports cover, principally, station identifications and frequencies used. They may include character, mode, and strength of signals; speed, time, and schedules of transmission; personal characteristics of observed operators; and other identifying information.

(2) Guarding missions include a constant watch on a designated frequency, copying or making sound recordings of all transmissions on those frequencies, and sending copies or recordings thereof to the control section.

c. *Control section.*—The platoon commander, through the control section, directs the operations of the intercept and position finding sections, consolidates information obtained by each, and forwards the consolidation to the company command post. In order that the control section may efficiently perform its function it is provided with personnel for a command team, a plotting station team, a wire construction team, and an administration team.

(1) The command team consists of the platoon commander and two assistant control chiefs. This team assigns missions to the intercept and position finding sections, supervises their installation and operations, and directs and supervises the activities of the other teams of the control section.

(2) The administration team consists of two clerks who assemble data from the intercept section and the plotting station team, and performs all other clerical tasks pertaining to the platoon.

(3) The wire construction team consists of a wire chief, two install-er-repairmen, and two linemen transported in a wire-laying vehicle. This team lays the wire circuit required for control of the direction finding stations of the platoon, installs the telephones required at these stations and at the control section, and may be required to construct a wire circuit to company headquarters or a tie-line to a circuit provided by higher headquarters.

(4) The plotting team consists of plotters who receive data from direction finding stations, prepare calibration correction charts, plot on maps the data received, and determine the position of the reported radio stations.

d. *Position finding section.*—This section consists of a section chief, an assistant section chief, and four direction finding station teams. Each team comprises a team chief and three radio operators. Each team is connected to the wire circuit laid by the wire construction team of the control section and one operator is employed as telephone orderly at the station. Stations operate direction finding equipment and receive targets or missions from and report azimuths to the control section. The section chief and the assistant chief reconnoiter for exact locations in which each station is to be installed, operate a vehicular radio transmitter during the preparation of calibration correction charts, and during operations serve at the control section as directed by the platoon commander.

■ 71. THEORY OF RADIO POSITION FINDING.—In order that the operations of the company may be more fully understood, an exposition of the elementary theory of radio position finding is presented in paragraphs 72 to 79. Rigorous mathematical analysis of this theory is beyond the scope of this manual. Only so much of the theory is presented as will provide an elementary understanding of position finding operations.

■ 72. DIRECTION FINDING.—It is possible to design an antenna which can be rotated so that its response to radio waves is greatest in one direction. It is also established that radio waves generally travel in great circle paths about the earth's surface. These two characteristics are employed in radio position finding to determine the absolute azimuth of a great circle arc joining a transmitter with the direction finding receiver. By the use of azimuths from two or more receivers, the location of a transmitter can be determined.

■ 73. ANTENNAS.—At the present time military direction finding receivers employ a combination of a loop and vertical antenna, or the Adcock antenna.

a. *Loop antenna.*—Signal voltages induced in a properly balanced loop antenna by a passing radio wave are canceled out when the plane of the loop is perpendicular to the direction of approach of the wave. Figure 18 shows the response pattern of a properly balanced loop. The lengths of the light arrowed lines indicate the relative response to waves arriving from the directions indicated. With the loop in the position shown in the figure, a wave of given strength will cause the greatest response when approaching from the direction of A or C, and the least response when approaching from B or D. If, therefore, a wave approaches from a given direction, and the loop is rotated so that its plane is at right angles to that direction, the response in the loop will be minimum, and the signal in the receiver to which the loop is connected will become very weak or disappear. The loop is then said to be in the "null" position with respect to that wave. The use of the null is a much more accurate method of direction determination than that of the point of maximum response, and is used exclusively in direction finding.

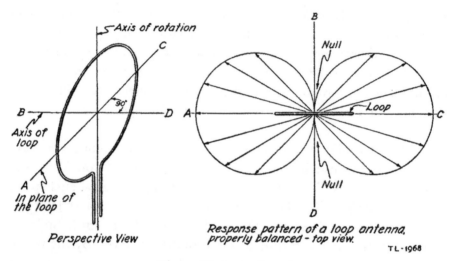

Figure 18. Loop antenna.

b. Sensing.—However, it can be seen in the figure that there are two null positions and that it is impossible using the loop alone to determine whether the wave is approaching from B or D. Through the use of a vertical antenna in combination with the loop it is possible to determine whether, as a matter of fact, the wave is approaching from B or D. This process of determination is known as sensing. As normally employed, the vertical antenna is mounted in the axis of rotation of the loop, as shown in figure 19. By properly adding the signal voltages induced by approaching waves in both the vertical antenna and in the loop, the response pattern of the combination is a cardioid with but one null position. It will be noted that this null is 90° away from those of the loop. Thus, with this combination, the loop may be rotated and a single null obtained for a given wave which will indicate its approximate but positive direction. In practice, after the direction of the wave has been sensed, the vertical antenna is disconnected from the circuit, and the loop is rotated to the position at which the original null was obtained. The proper azimuth is then read. This azimuth (determined from the use of loop alone) is employed because a crisper and more accurate null can be obtained than that by using the combination of the loop and vertical antenna. In the practical application of the loop to military direction finding equipment provision is made for careful orientation of the loop to true north for azimuth readings, or to a given base line. Provision for reception of all types of transmission, properly balancing the loop, obtaining nulls, "sensing," and interconnecting with other direction finding stations for a comparison of signals being received are all included.

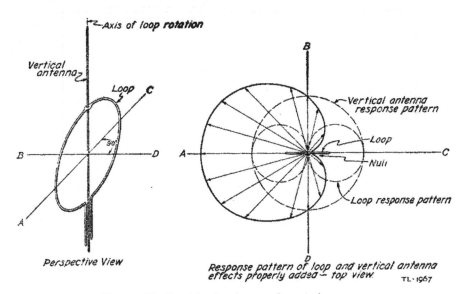

Figure 19. Combination loop and vertical antenna.

c. *Adcock antennas.*—Types of antennas developed by Adcock, one of which is illustrated in figure 20, are designed so that only the vertical members of the antennas are effective, and the horizontal members are rendered ineffective either by shielding or by neutralizing them electrically. This type of antenna, perfectly balanced, has a figure-eight response pattern similar to that of the loop antenna, and may be operated for direction finding in a like manner as that for the loop. The Adcock antenna has particular usefulness for direction finding of radio waves of above 3,000 kc. in frequency.

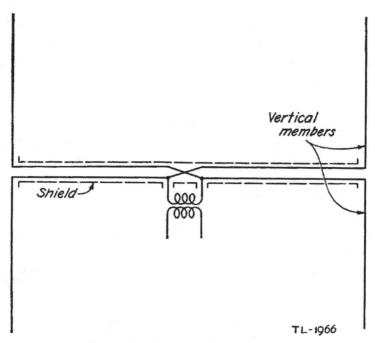

Figure 20. One type of Adcock antenna.

CHAPTER 4

Aerial Intelligence
and Naval Intelligence

Aerial intelligence—by which we mainly refer to the gathering of intelligence via aerial photo-reconnaissance—became one of the most powerful tools in the American intelligence arsenal during World War II. In fact, the historian Sebastian Cox has identified photo-reconnaissance as second only to signals intelligence as the most important intelligence source in the war. The influence of this mode of intelligence gathering was the outcome of several technological advancements. The development of increasingly capable monoplanes during the 1930s and 1940s gave world armies the ideal platforms for mounting powerful aerial cameras. During the war the most effective U.S. reconnaissance aircraft were the P-38 Lightning and P-51 Mustang, as these were capable of high speeds and twisting maneuverability, which in the absence of armament (most photo-reconnaissance aircraft were unarmed) aided their survivability, plus they could operate confidently at both low levels and high altitudes. Camera technology also became sophisticated in both resolution and configuration. By 1942, photo-reconnaissance cameras were capable of taking 1:10,000 scale images from 30,000ft (9,150m), and stereoscopic techniques meant that interpreters could view three-dimensional images. Between 1942 and 1944, U.S. aviators photographed a total of 8 million square miles (21 million square km) of land, and such was the value of photo reconnaissance to the intelligence effort that General Henry "Hap" Arnold, commander of the U.S. Army Air Forces, once stated that "a camera mounted on a P-38 often has proved of more value than a P-38 with guns."

The first manual in this chapter, Intelligence Procedure in Aviation Units, *was published by the U.S. Army Air Corps in 1940, before the United States was dragged into the conflict. Partly on account of American research*

The F-6 Mustang was a photo-reconnaissance version of the P-51 Mustang fighter aircraft. It carried two K-24 cameras. (U.S. Air National Guard)

into British photographic intelligence operations between 1939 and 1940, it already demonstrates a strong awareness of the technologies and capabilities of photo reconnaissance.

★★★

From FM 1-40, *Air Corps Field Manual: Intelligence Procedure in Aviation Units* (1940)

CHAPTER 2
INTELLIGENCE PROCEDURE WITH GHQ AVIATION

Section 1
GENERAL

[. . .]

■ 13. NORMAL SEQUENCE.—*a*. The functions of an intelligence officer on the staff of an air commander follow a routine sequence and when viewed as a whole illustrate a coordinated and continuing process.

b. A sequence or cycle of intelligence procedure for any specific tactical mission may be as follows:

NOTE.—In the following outline, actions by the intelligence officer are shown in italics, whereas corresponding actions of the air commander, other members of his staff, or by the air combat units themselves are in plain type.

(1) *Prior to the tactical employment of an air combat unit, the intelligence officer of the unit will receive from the commander of the field forces through proper channels, all the War Department intelligence available upon the theater of operations and/or bearing upon the general mission to which that particular air unit is assigned. He may also have produced some preliminary combat intelligence from information collected from early reconnaissance.*

(2) The commander of the air combat unit to which the intelligence officer is assigned (henceforth referred to as the air commander) receives an order from higher authority assigning a tactical mission. The air commander makes a commander's estimate of the situation considering therein certain factors that may affect his mission.

(3) *The intelligence officer assists his commander in making the commander's estimate by furnishing him as completely as possible intelligence on the following factors:*

(*a*) *Exact location and description of the objective and arrangement of targets therein. This will be in the form of objective folders except in the case of fleeting objectives.*

(*b*) *Strength, disposition, and effectiveness of hostile air and ground antiaircraft defenses at and en route to and from the objective, and the enemy situation and capabilities as they affect the air attack of the objective. This will be furnished in the form of an intelligence estimate of the situation.*

(*c*) *Weather conditions at and en route to and from the objective in the form of a route forecast obtained from the weather service.*

(4) The air commander now announces to his staff his decision and his directive for the plan of operation of his unit in carrying out the mission assigned him. Also at this time, he announces those additional

items of information regarding the objective, enemy's capabilities as to influencing the conduct of the mission, and weather conditions which he must have to conduct the operation he has decided upon.

(5) *The intelligence officer frames the needed items of information into clear and concisely stated essential elements of information and recommends them to his commander to be published as such.*

(6) The air commander designates these essential elements of information with any modifications he may make and causes them to be published to the command. He then directs the intelligence officer to instruct all available information collecting agencies to concentrate upon the collection of these essential elements of information.

(7) *Based upon the framework of the essential elements of information and in conformity with the air commander's directive, the intelligence officer prepares the intelligence plan for the collection of information. He coordinates this with other members of the staff, especially the operations officer, and presents it for the air commander's approval.*

(8) The air commander approves the intelligence plan with any modifications he may desire and directs the intelligence officer to issue the necessary instructions to collecting agencies to put the plan into effect.

(9) *The intelligence officer consolidates the instructions to each collecting agency and immediately issues them in the form of intelligence orders to each subordinate agency and in the form of requests to higher, neighboring, and cooperating units. Likewise he prepares the Intelligence Annex, if necessary, to accompany the field order.*

(10) As a result of the receipt of the intelligence orders above, the several collecting agencies obtain and forward to the intelligence officer items of enemy information, especially such items as bear directly on the essential elements.

(11) *The intelligence officer receives the incoming information, recording it in the intelligence journal; collates the information, using the intelligence work sheet; evaluates the information; and interprets the information, reducing it into usable concise items of combat intelligence. He then disseminates this combat intelligence*

in any or all of the following ways to the air commander and to higher, lower, neighboring, and cooperating unit commanders:

(a) By personal contact, special messages to, or conferences with intelligence officers of units concerned.

(b) By posting it on intelligence situation map.

(c) By presenting a new intelligence estimate of the situation to the air commander and staff.

(d) By issuing a periodic intelligence report.

(e) By issuing special intelligence reports and intelligence studies.

(f) By issuing an intelligence summary to units concerned.

(g) By issuing objective folders as received from higher headquarters, or by issuing photographs, overlays, diagrams, or written changes or additions to specific

Civilian photo technicians (in the back of the jeep) working for the Counter Intelligence Corps pass through a security check point in Potsdam, Germany, in July 1945. (NARA)

objective folders already issued; or by initiating new objective folders upon the discovery of new objectives.

(h) By field orders and intelligence annexes thereto.

★★★

The chief value of aerial photo reconnaissance was the way in which the images produced could be put to a multitude of uses. They could aid high-level strategic decisions, providing a bird's eye view of the enemy's economic and logistical infrastructure while identifying targets for tactical air strikes or strategic bombing. They could give insight into the enemy's operational plans; although an individual photograph was a static image, comparison between time-staged photographs could indicate troop, train, or vehicle movements. A good set of aerial photographs might provide a U.S. commander with that vital bit of information sufficient to make the difference between a successful attack or a calamitous defeat. It could tell a naval commander just what enemy vessels were in reach of his fleet or force. As the following manual implies, however, the key to putting together a successful photo-reconnaissance mission lay in matching the right technology for the job with a sound operational plan. Aerial intelligence operations needed planning with all the rigor of combat missions if they were to yield the best results.

★★★

From FM 30-21, *War Department Field Manual: Aerial Photography Military Applications* (1944)

SECTION II
AERIAL PHOTOGRAPHS

■ 4. DEFINITIONS. *a.* An aerial photograph is a picture, either vertical or oblique, taken from an aircraft. The average person is unaccustomed to an aerial viewpoint and therefore the images of familiar objects on aerial photographs appear strange and unassociated with the objects represented. The difficulties presented in interpretation of aerial photography are such that special training in its use is required if the maximum value is to be obtained therefrom.

b. Classes of aerial photography are:

(1) *Intelligence.* Aerial photographic information of terrain, activities, or installations.

(2) *Mapping and charting.* Aerial photographs used in the compilation and correction of topographic and planimetric maps, photomaps, models, aeronautical and hydrographic charts of all types.

(3) *Bombardment.* Orientation photography of terrain at time of bombing release and bomb impact photography to show location of bomb bursts with respect to target.

■ 5. CAMERA TYPES. Aerial cameras are of two types; reconnaissance and mapping. Mapping cameras are necessarily related to the requirements of the topographic organization (TM 5-240). Reconnaissance cameras include a variety of focal lengths, angles of coverage, and types of shutters in order to provide the classes of photography required.

■ 6. VERTICALS. A vertical aerial photograph is one made with the camera axis vertical or as nearly vertical as practicable in an aircraft. Figure 1 shows a vertical photograph. The area shown on this photograph is represented within the rectangle in figure 3. The camera film is practically horizontal at exposure, hence features on the ground are registered on a vertical photograph in perspective with minimum distortion of their horizontal dimensions.

Figure 1. Vertical photograph of rectangular area of Figure 3.

■ 7. OBLIQUES. Oblique aerial photographs are obtained by tilting the optical axis of the camera from the vertical. Figure 2 is a reproduction of an oblique photograph. This oblique photograph covers an area represented by the trapezoidal section of the map marked on figure 3.

Figure 2. Oblique photograph of area shown by trapezoid of Figure 3.

Figure 3. Rectangular area in foreground indicates coverage of vertical photograph of Figure 1. Entire trapezoid show coverage of oblique photograph of Figure 2.

■ 8. SCALE. Scale is the relationship between a distance on a map or photograph and the actual distance on the ground. This is usually expressed as a ratio called the representative fraction (RF). The scale of a photograph is established by the focal length of the lens used and the altitude of the camera at the time of the exposure.

■ 9. MARGINAL DATA. Certain information will appear on the margin of photographic prints. These marginal data include geographic location, time and date of the photography, and other necessary reference data. Marginal data are prescribed in Army Air Forces Regulation 95-7 and are set forth in *Photo Interpretation Handbook—U.S. Forces*. These prescribed data have War Department approval as meeting all Army requirements and must be adhered to.

■ 10. PRINT PAPER. *a*. Photographs may be printed on either glossy, matte, or semimatte paper of single or double weight. Glossy paper gives clearest definition of detail and is normally used for photo interpretation. The other types are used for special purposes.

b. Print papers with a water-resistant base are for quick work and for production printing. They have a comparatively glossy surface and are suitable for photo interpretation. These papers are not intended for mosaic production.

■ 11. STEREOSCOPIC COVERAGE. When a detailed study of an object is to be undertaken, it is necessary to secure overlapping photographs that may be studied with a stereoscope. Most reconnaissance photography is planned in this manner. Two such overlapping photographs are called a "stereoscopic pair." Mapping photography also requires stereoscopic coverage.

■ 12. RECONNAISSANCE STRIPS. *a*. A reconnaissance strip is a series of overlapping photographs made from an airplane flying a selected course. Vertical photographs are usually taken in such strips with a minimum overlap of 60 percent of the successive exposures forming the strip.

b. Oblique reconnaissance strip photographs may be made in similar fashion with consistent overlapping when oblique mounts are installed in the aircraft.

■ 13. MOSAICS AND PHOTOMAPS. *a.* Uncontrolled mosaic. An uncontrolled mosaic is formed by joining several overlapping vertical photographs taken at different camera positions. The term is generally applied to an assembly of one or more vertical strips. When the several photographs are oriented with respect to each other, the result is an "uncontrolled mosaic." This provides a good pictorial representation of the ground, but will have errors in scale and azimuth.

b. Controlled mosaic. When the several photographs are brought to a uniform scale, oriented with respect to one another and fitted to points of ground control, the result is a "controlled mosaic." The accuracy of a controlled mosaic used as a map depends upon the quality of the photography, the character and amount of ground control, and the methods used in its preparation.

c. Photomaps. A reproduction of a photograph or mosaic upon which grid lines, marginal data, and place names are ordinarily added is called a "photomap" and may be reproduced in quantity by photographic or lithographic methods.

[. . .]

SECTION IV

PHOTOGRAPHIC RECONNAISSANCE OPERATIONS

■ 19. GENERAL. *a.* The mission of photographic aviation is to secure and produce for military operations of the armed forces—

(1) Photographic reconnaissance information.

(2) Map and chart information.

b. Modern aerial photography is highly specialized. [. . .] It is sufficient in this manual to observe that the best photography for a specific purpose can be produced only if the primary purpose for which it is intended is made known to those who accomplish the photography, as well as to those who are required to interpret it.

■ 20. RECONNAISSANCE PHOTOGRAPHY. Aerial photographs are one of the most important sources of information available to a commander and when successfully interpreted frequently reveal the most carefully guarded secrets in hostile territory. They reveal enemy transportation and communication systems; port and harbor facilities; industrial installations and activities; air, ground, and naval installations and activities. Such information is of utmost importance to all echelons of command both for planning and execution of operations against the enemy.

■ 21. TYPES OF UNITS. Reconnaissance aviation provides two types of organizations for the initial procurement of aerial photography: photo reconnaissance units and tactical reconnaissance units.

    a. Photo reconnaissance units. The photo reconnaissance units operate normally at high altitudes and long range in cooperation with units operating strategically. They are trained and equipped to obtain reconnaissance photography as well as mapping and charting photography. They usually operate unarmed, depending upon speed, altitude, and evasive tactics for protection. In certain theaters, appropriate bombardment type aircraft are employed consistent with the ranges required. These bomber type aircraft may be armed. Photographic reconnaissance aircraft are normally equipped with cameras of 6-, 24-, and 40-inch focal lengths.

    b. Tactical reconnaissance units. The tactical reconnaissance units normally operate at extremely low or medium altitudes in cooperation with units operating tactically, and obtain both photographic and visual information to facilitate the proper employment of the tactical air, ground, and amphibious forces. Photographic equipment of tactical reconnaissance units limits them to taking obliques, verticals, and photographic strips of limited areas. Combination visual and photographic tactical reconnaissance missions are customary. A flash report is sent on the visual information with an interpretation report and photographs following. Additional photographic requirements, beyond the capabilities of the tactical reconnaissance units, are requested of the photographic reconnaissance organization.

■ 22. OPERATIONAL CONSIDERATIONS FOR RECONNAISSANCE PHOTOGRAPHY. [. . .] It should be noted that the success of the photo reconnaissance mission depends to a great extent upon clarity and precision of the request for photography. The problem parallels that of procurement of

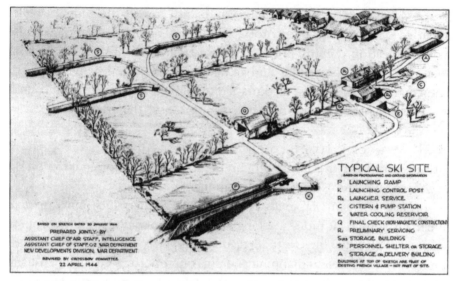

A U.S. intelligence diagram of a V–1 flying bomb "ski site." (U.S. Air Force)

information by ground patrols and is further complicated by the possibility of mechanical failure, vulnerability incident to the necessity for operation within view of the enemy, and, within limits, weather conditions. In the employment of aerial photography as source of information the following is necessary:

a. Technical requirements of the photography to meet the specific purposes must be defined.

b. Objectives or areas to be photographed must be accurately described.

c. When appropriate, prior to the dispatch of a photo reconnaissance mission, a check is made of existing photography to determine to what extent the information or photography is available.

d. If a mission is necessary the following steps must be taken: (1) Priorities for the accomplishment of photographic missions must be established. (2) Aircraft equipped with suitable photographic facilities must be flown over the selected objectives; film must be exposed under conditions that will meet technical photographic requirements; and the aircraft must return to its base. (3) The exposed film must be developed, printed, and interpreted to extract all pertinent information.

■ 23. Bomb Impact Photography. On most operational bombardment missions, a certain number of bomber aircraft are equipped with cameras which expose film during the bombing missions. This photography normally shows point of bomb release and is useful in developing bomb impact plots. Under certain conditions, it is possible to accredit particular bomb bursts to individual aircraft. The principal value of bomb impact photography is the immediate indication of the success of the mission. As detail of the target is obscured by smoke from bomb explosions, bomb impact photography is not satisfactory for bomb damage assessment. Its chief use is for operational studies.

■ 24. Damage Assessment Photography. As soon as practicable, reconnaissance is dispatched to procure photography to be used in the assessment of damage. This photography is normally accomplished by reconnaissance aircraft. Similarly, in tactical reconnaissance, photography is accomplished for the same purpose after artillery bombardment. Damage assessment determines the point beyond which further bombardment is no longer necessary, and permits an estimate of the probable damage that will be caused by similar missions against similar targets. It is also useful in long range intelligence to determine enemy capabilities.

■ 25. Night Photography. *a.* Night photography is accomplished with special cameras using light from high intensity flash bombs or other sources. Proper appreciation of night photography should be based on the special technical problems involved:

(1) The candlepower of the light source limits the area which may be illuminated.

(2) The number of photographs that may be made on any individual mission will depend upon the type of light source used.

(3) Precise navigation at night may be extremely difficult.

b. Information derived from the interpretation of night photographs includes—

(1) *Reconnaissance.* The detection of the night activities of the enemy such as movement of troops, batteries, shipping, and supplies.

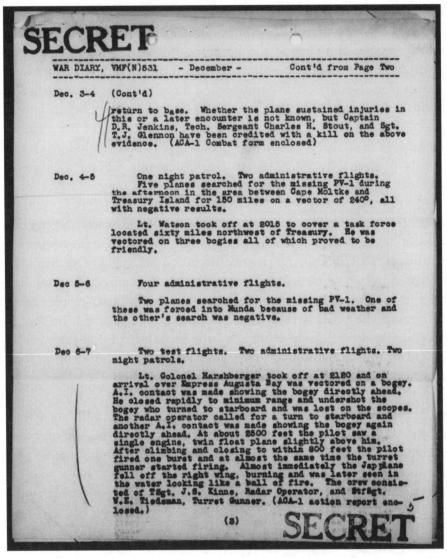

SECRET

WAR DIARY, VMF(N)531   - December -   Cont'd from Page Two

Dec. 3-4   (Cont'd)

return to base. Whether the plane sustained injuries in
this or a later encounter is not known, but Captain
D.R. Jenkins, Tech. Sergeant Charles H. Stout, and Sgt.
T.J. Glennon have been credited with a kill on the above
evidence. (ACA-1 Combat form enclosed)

Dec. 4-5   One night patrol. Two administrative flights.
           Five planes searched for the missing PV-1 during
the afternoon in the area between Cape Moltke and
Treasury Island for 150 miles on a vector of 240°, all
with negative results.

           Lt. Watson took off at 2015 to cover a task force
located sixty miles northwest of Treasury. He was
vectored on three bogies all of which proved to be
friendly.

Dec 5-6   Four administrative flights.

           Two planes searched for the missing PV-1. One of
these was forced into Munda because of bad weather and
the other's search was negative.

Dec 6-7   Two test flights. Two administrative flights. Two
night patrols.

           Lt. Colonel Harshberger took off at 2120 and on
arrival over Empress Augusta Bay was vectored on a bogey.
A.I. contact was made showing the bogey directly ahead.
He closed rapidly to minimum range and undershot the
bogey who turned to starboard and was lost on the scopes.
The radar operator called for a turn to starboard and
another A.I. contact was made showing the bogey again
directly ahead. At about 2500 feet the pilot saw a
single engine, twin float plane slightly above him.
After climbing and closing to within 800 feet the pilot
fired one burst and at almost the same time the turret
gunner started firing. Almost immediately the Jap plane
fell off the right wing, burning and was later seen in
the water looking like a ball of fire. The crew consisted of TSgt. J.S. Kinne, Radar Operator, and StfSgt.
W.E. Tiedeman, Turret Gunner. (ACA-1 action report enclosed.)

(3)

SECRET

Pages from a classified war diary produced by Marine Night Fighter Squadron 531
(VMF(N)-531) (USMC).

(2) *Bombardment*. Photographs from individual aircraft establish the
exact position of the attack when compared with daylight reconnaissance
photographs or accurate maps of the area under attack. All of the
photographs taken by the various aircraft of the mission when studied
together indicate the overall effect of the mission.

■ 26. COLOR PHOTOGRAPHY. Aerial color photography has recently reached a stage of development where it may be of practical operational value. It has been of some value for the study of offshore and beach conditions and in the detection and interpretation of camouflaged or otherwise concealed installations. The limiting factors associated with the use of aerial color photography include the necessity of viewing transparencies and the difficulties incident to reproduction.

■ 27. INFRA RED PHOTOGRAPHY. Infra red photography is taken on special film and has very limited application in theaters of operation. It may be of value in camouflage detection of installations concealed with ordinary paints or dyed cloth or imitative vegetation.

■ 28. LIMITATIONS OF AERIAL PHOTOGRAPHY. *a.* The uses to which aerial photographs may be put depend upon the technical quality of the photograph. This quality in turn is dependent upon the following:
(1) Light conditions.
(2) Weather.
(3) Characteristics of the equipment.
(4) Ability of the pilot.
(5) Ability of the laboratory personnel.
b. The processes of photography all require time for their accomplishment. Time is required for each of the several steps of processing negatives and prints and interpretation of photos, as well as for the mechanics of preparing for, performance of, and return from the aerial mission. The requester, the airdrome, and the photographic laboratory and interpretation section may be separated by such distances as will involve a considerable expenditure of time. This time factor must be considered by all who request aerial photographs.
c. Successful interpretation depends upon the skill and experiences of the individual interpreter, the reference material available to him, the quality of the photographs, the scale of the photographs, and the time available for interpretation. In general the better the quality of the photograph, the smaller the scale at which a specific type of installation can be accurately interpreted. Detailed interpretation calls for a scale as large as possible consistent with the equipment available and safety

A U.S. intelligence officer checks off the names of the pilots after they had returned from a mission over Guadalcanal in June 1943. (U.S. Army Signal Corps)

of flight. Mapping and general preliminary planning can be done with photographs of smaller scale.

★★★

The interpretation of aerial photographs in World War II was a mix of art, analysis, and technical knowledge. Although camera technologies had improved considerably since the beginning of the century, the images they produced could still be grainy, cloud-misted affairs, the details on the land further obscured and complicated by tricks of light or contour. Added to these challenges was the fact that the enemy being photographed often implemented countermeasures to pho-to-reconnaissance, such as overhead camouflage. Thus, photographic interpretation required a highly analytical mind, often trusting more to logical deductions rather than instinctive responses to visual appearances. TM 5-246, Interpretation of Aerial Photographs *gives some insight into this world, instructing the trainee or intelligence officer what to look for in the images that sat under their magnifying and measuring equipment.*

★★★

From TM 5-246, *Interpretation of Aerial Photographs* (1942)

Chapter 2
MILITARY INTERPRETATION

Section I
GENERAL

33. Purpose and scope.—*a.* The purpose of this chapter is to teach interpretation of military activity as shown on aerial photographs. Most of the vehicles, equipment, formations, and installations shown in the figures are those of the United States Army because the student must learn interpretation by studying items of that nature which are familiar to him. When he has become proficient; in identifying these, it will be fairly easy for him to extend his knowledge to similar enemy equipment and installations.

b. This chapter covers interpretation of aerial photographs of military activities in the theater of operations. It will serve as a guide to student interpreters who work with the ground and supporting air forces. Large rear air bases and industrial and shipping installations in the zone of the interior are an aerial photographic study so different as to warrant a separate text and therefore will not be included in this manual.

34. Photographs in war.—*a. Types.*—War photographs fall into three main classes: vertical, high oblique, and low oblique. With the use of a long focal length camera, large-scale photographs can be obtained at extremely high altitudes. Sharp obliques at low altitudes may be obtained by mounting a camera so as to take the oblique along the axis of the airplane.

b. Interpreter and photographer.—Close cooperation between the interpreter and the aerial photographer is of great importance. If the interpreter is to obtain maximum efficiency, he must have a thorough understanding of the limitations of the photographer and his equipment. He must keep abreast of all changes in equipment, enemy interference, and efficiency of photographic personnel. Whenever possible, the photographer should give the interpreter information he remembers from visual observation. He should also specify the priority of printing special negatives in the roll of film which he has exposed.

35. Photographic missions.—*a. General.*—A photographic mission should be ordered for specific information in a specified area. Specifications, such as the exact scale of the photographs, should be advisory only. The photographic agency should be told what specific information is desired but should be allowed to determine the best method for accomplishing its mission with the available facilities. Examples of missions are to obtain photographs of all bridges, fords, or ferries crossing a particular river between two specified points; to photograph an entire area in which activity has been discovered in order to determine the specific nature of the activity.

b. Missions for specific studies.—In cases where missions over enemy territory are ordered for specific studies, such as routes of advance of an armored unit or location of hostile artillery, the requirements should be completely outlined. For routes of advance of the armored force, photographs are desired which afford studies of size and probable capacities of bridges, the steepness of river banks, and the depth of water in streams which are probably fordable. For the study of artillery positions, photographs of probable locations such as woods bordered by fields or roads, defiladed positions, and hedges are desired. These studies require good stereo pairs and often require low obliques.

36. Recording photographs.—When photographs are first received they are usually identified by mission number and date. As soon as the location of the photograph is determined it should be marked with the proper geographical identification, and eventually filed by this identification. The information sought by the mission on which the photograph was taken may become useless in a short time, but the photographed area may be rephotographed at a later date and the earlier photograph become priceless for comparative purposes. A file system should be developed to fit best the maps used in the area. The general sector of operation should be divided into smaller sections; squares of about 20,000 yards should prove appropriate. All photographs within this area should be filed together in chronological order. In case a photograph includes two areas, a copy should be placed in each file. The area mentioned should conform to coordinates and a small-scale master map should give the immediate location of a given area. Where the position is stabilized, smaller areas may be used for filing. All photographs should be given a geographical file number as soon as the first phase interpretation has been made.

37. First phase interpretation.—This phase of interpretation covers that activity which will require immediate countermeasures and which affects the day-by-day conduct of the war. Since landing fields are usually some distance from the headquarters of a ground unit, it is desirable that a good first phase interpretation be accomplished at the photographic laboratory near the landing field. This first phase interpretation is conducted with the assistance of the photographers. It results in processing photographs which are more likely to contain desirable information before those of less value. Information derived from the first phase interpretation may occasionally be transmitted rapidly to the ground force before all photographs obtained on the mission are completely processed.

38. Second phase interpretation.—*a. General.*—When the outstanding information has been obtained from photographs and a geographical file number has been designated, second phase interpretation is started. This phase includes a thorough search of every photograph to determine the existence of any military information. It should be done at the headquarters of the ground force because—

(1) The ground force can make full use of its knowledge concerning the rapidly changing military situation.

(2) Other sources of information are available for rapid verification.

(3) The appearance of new enemy installations or equipment is appreciated more because of ground contact with them.

b. Transparencies.—A type of second phase interpretation which may be simultaneously accomplished at the photograph laboratory is the careful study of selected photographs by viewing positive transparencies. The organic equipment within the laboratory allows these studies, and in some cases more detail can be seen from the transparency. Under certain conditions a color photograph gives more detail and contrast than a black and white photograph. Color transparencies can be obtained when the weather is suitable, and the interpretation made at the photographic laboratory.

39. Obliques.—In some cases the ground forces may request that obliques be taken over enemy lines at low altitudes, where verticals would be impracticable due to slow film and shutter speeds being unable to "stop" the ground. The lower units of the ground forces will find much use for obliques of enemy territory which are taken from behind our lines. These obliques may be reproduced by lithography in great quantity for wide distribution and can be used by company officers for studying terrain to their front. The interpreters may be called on to give instruction in their use.

40. Stereo studies.—Stereo studies are necessary for tactical interpretation. The principles of stereo vision are explained in FM 21-26 and in other manuals. Single photographs appear throughout this manual, but it is due primarily to the difficulty of presenting in book form photographs for stereo study. Stereo pairs or triplets are the rule rather than the exception for interpretation studies. The use of single photographs for training is discouraged.

41. Interpretation equipment.—*a. Necessary equipment.*—In the study of photographs for intelligence purposes a small portion of the photograph is viewed at one time. While the map maker is interested in terrain features and their physical relation to each other, and for this reason needs a stereoscope with wide coverage, the tactical interpreter concentrates upon objects of extremely small size; hence, in most cases, a pocket stereoscope meets his requirements. Other equipment commonly used in intelligence interpretation is an illuminating magnifying glass, 1:100 inch or 1:1,000 foot scales (may be special scales to fit magnifying glass), grease pencils, books on close studies of equipment, and maps.

b. Other equipment.—In large interpretation units other equipment such as magnifying mirror stereoscopes, parallax measuring devices (height finders), and shadow charts is found.

(1) The magnifying mirror stereoscope accomplishes little in interpretation work that cannot be accomplished with the small pocket stereoscope.

(2) Parallax measuring devices such as Abram contour finder, Talley-Fairchild stereo-comparagraph and binocular stereoscope with parallax bar

may be used to find the elevation of one point or object above another. This equipment has its limitations, for serious errors will result in the determination of elevations by parallax measurements on photographs tilted as little as 1° or 2°. [. . .]

(3) Shadow charts are used to determine the height of an object when the length of its shadow can be measured. Charts can be made up for an area by determining the length of shadows of objects of known heights for each hour of the day. As shadow lengths vary with the time of day, geographical location, and time of year, these variables must be considered. Shadows must fall on fairly even ground to have their lengths accurately measured for height determinations.

[. . .]

Section IV
CAMPS AND BIVOUACS

47. Location and identification.—*a. Camps.*—Semipermanent camps may be found in enemy rear areas. They will probably be near towns or villages where utilities are accessible and may be located near air bases and seacoast installations. The presence of one will usually disclose the others.

b. Bivouacs.—Near the battle line, highly dispersed bivouacs are of little value in interpretation since they present no particular target. In rear areas where reserves and fast moving units are located, however, the identification of bivouacs is extremely important. They often give the key to the enemy intentions by disclosing the locations of his concentrations. Photographs of such mobile units as an armored force are of little value except when they are in bivouac. In general, bivouacs may be expected in areas that provide the best—

(1) Concealment for men and equipment from aerial and terrestrial observation.

(2) Means of dispersion. Large forces will not be grouped in small, isolated woods.

(3) Communication. An area will be sought which contains an existing road net.

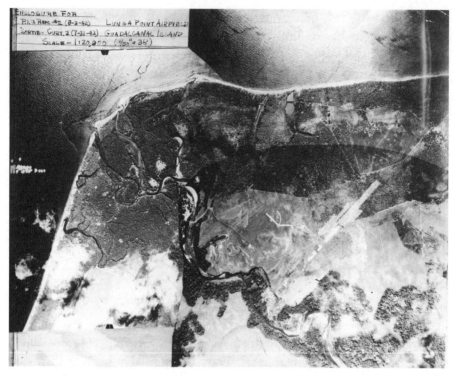

Aerial reconnaissance photo of Lunga Point, Guadalcanal on July 31, 1942.

(4) Protection against attack—in the vicinity of natural obstacles, where possible.

(5) Water supply, especially in an arid country.

c. Means of identification.—Bivouacs are detected by the following, listed in order of importance:

(1) Tracks of vehicles.

(2) Vehicles.

(3) "Trashy" appearance, caused by small and personal equipment.

(4) "Worn" spots—change in texture due to human and vehicular traffic.

(5) Tentage and personnel.

48. Command posts.—Command posts of large units will be found generally in existing buildings in towns or villages. When vehicles are kept under cover, these command posts are difficult to locate. Where there are few villages, command posts are located in farm buildings or in woods. In interpreting photographs, farm buildings adjoining heavy woods should be viewed with suspicion since there is usually room for

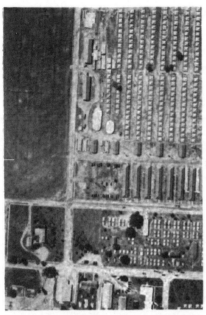 

FIGURE 127.—Scale 1:3,500: A day photograph, taken about noon, is shown for comparison with the adjoining night photograph of the same area.

FIGURE 128.—Scale 1:3,500: Night photograph of a camp. Though detail is blurred, note that any general feature can be identified. Drainage features are easily recognized.

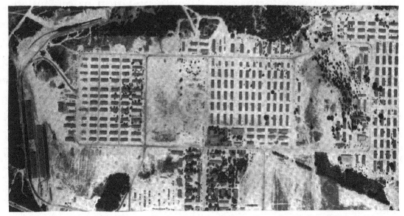

FIGURE 129.—Scale 1:10,000: Large permanent camp of cantonment type. This cantonment area is sufficient to quarter, except for hospitalization, approximately 10,000 men.

a command post, an entering road and turn-around, and cover for the attached troops and installations.

[. . .]

51. Length of occupation.—The interpreter can, in some cases, make an estimation of the length of time a bivouac has been occupied. Constant study of bivouacs of our own forces is the best means of becoming proficient in this estimation. The significant features in the study of length of occupation are:

(1) Tracks, paths, and roads compared with terrain in the vicinity unoccupied by military forces.

(2) Excavation or fortifications existing within the occupied area.

(3) Differences in general texture of earth in vicinity.

[. . .]

SECTION V
TROOP MOVEMENTS

52. Value of photographs of troop movements.—*a. Identification of unit*.—Though a unit may be miles from where it is photographed by the time the information gets to higher headquarters the knowledge that a certain type of force is moving at a certain speed in a certain direction still remains valuable information. All interpretation of movements on the road must be first phase interpretation at the photographic laboratory, and may be made entirely from negatives.

b. Time element.—An interval of 2 to 4 hours or longer may elapse between the photographing of a moving unit and the time the interpreted data reach higher headquarters. In 2 to 4 hours units may cover distances as shown in the following table:

Troop unit	Miles per hour slowest vehicle in column travels	Miles column has probably traveled		
		2 hours	3 hours	4 hours
Men marching	2½	5	7.5	10
Field artillery, animal	3½	7	10.5	14
Cavalry (horse)	6	12	18	24
Motors	10	20	30	40
Motors	35	70	105	140

c. Aid to future identification.—Photographs of troop movements are also of value to interpreters at the ground force headquarters for use in identifying equipment. Equipment on an open road is in the best location for study from an aerial photograph. By comparison, the same equipment may be identified in a later photograph in which the equipment is half hidden in woods.

53. Identification of units.—*a. Importance.*—Units, like vehicles, are much easier to identify on the road than in bivouac. If a unit can be photographed on the road and later photographed or observed going into bivouac, the interpreter's problem is greatly reduced. The aerial observer may report the photographing of a column at a certain time and location, and this information may be radioed direct from airplane to headquarters, but information as to the size and type of force may not be available until the interpreter has had time to view the negatives or perhaps the prints.

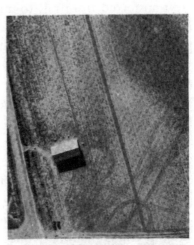

FIGURE 196.—Scale 1:2,000: This photograph shows truck tracks. Note that the turning radii are larger and more even than those of tanks, and also the tracks are not as deeply cut. These differences can usually be seen on photographs of any scale.

FIGURE 195.—Scale 1:2,000: Photograph showing tank tracks. Note the sharp turning radii and the deeply gouged turns caused by braking one track. Tank tracks are usually more wavy than those of trucks.

b. Means.—Weapons on towed or self-propelled mounts and distinctive vehicles or mobile equipment are the only means of identifying a unit on the road. When the identifying features cannot be distinguished, as is common to extremely small-scale photographs, the speed of travel may be some indication as to the type of unit. Speed is determined from the time interval and the distance a vehicle has traveled between successive photographs.

[. . .]

SECTION VI
SUPPLY INSTALLATIONS

56. Railheads and dumps.—*a. Railheads.*—Points where supplies are transferred from rail to another type of transportation are called railheads. A railhead may be established for any or all classes of supplies. The essential facilities of a railhead are sidings for unloading of supplies, a road net adjacent thereto suitable for operation of motorized trains, and storage space for such reserves as may be maintained. When supplies are stored, the railhead may also be called a dump. Railheads are generally found in small towns and cities where sidings and storage space already exist. Where possible, an attempt is made to select a site for a railhead that affords the best existing protection and concealment; this may be supplemented by camouflage, antiaircraft, or other defensive means.

b. Dumps.—Dumps are temporary stocks of military supplies. Generally, a dump will contain only one class of supplies and will vary from large facilities in rear areas to small piles of supplies in forward areas. Different classes of supplies will often have characteristic arrangements for storage; for example, an ammunition dump will be dispersed and away from other activities. When supplies are issued from dumps, they become distributing points.

c. Identification.—(1) Railheads in towns are identified by existing traffic and signs of abnormal activity. In the theater of operations civilian activity decreases appreciably.

(2) Dumps, though well concealed, are usually identified by tracks and new roads. It is difficult to conceal the evidence of heavy traffic.

57. Water points.—*a. Requirements.*—Water points must have a source of water and be accessible from a main supply road. They should be protected and concealed. There should be a concealed place for waiting vehicles. There must be adequate space for pumping, purification, loading, and storage facilities, and for traffic past the area.

b. Identification.—Since trucks generally line up waiting to be loaded with water, the best time to issue water is at night. Little traffic around a water point near the battle line may be expected in daylight. In night driving, less care is given to camouflage discipline, and for this reason the turn-off from the main supply road may be in evidence on a daylight photograph. Thus, to locate an enemy water point, roads are carefully examined for turn-offs where they cross streams or pass near lakes. In

A U.S. B-24 overflies a Japanese-controlled bridge in Burma.

towns, the local water supply systems will be used. In the case of a destroyed town, the vicinity of the original source of water supply for the town should be examined on a photograph to determine whether or not the source has been improved for military use.

Section VII
ANTIAIRCRAFT POSITIONS

58. Location.—*a. Tactically.*—In the combat zone, antiaircraft artillery will be found protecting bivouacs, troops on the march, military operations such as river crossings, supply and administrative establishments, and routes of communication. In the rear areas, antiaircraft weapons will be found protecting such installations as mobilization centers, regulating stations, airdromes, naval bases, shipping points, and manufacturing centers.

b. Technically.—The principal requirement for locating antiaircraft weapons to perform their primary mission of defense against air attack is an unobstructed field of fire through 360° in azimuth. The larger caliber antiaircraft artillery (3-inch and 90-mm) will be found usually 1,000 to 3,000 yards from the object or area it is defending, and in a location where it can fire to a minimum elevation of 10° to 15°. This means that the guns will be located in positions near crests of hills, at the foot of gentle slopes, and in small orchards, underbrush, cornfields, and grain fields. Another requirement is that they must be in the vicinity of good roads, with routes leading in all directions. The automatic weapons (37-mm and cal. .50 machine guns) will be found in similar locations, 200 to 500 yards from the object or area they are defending.

59. Identification.—The 3-inch and 90-mm antiaircraft batteries consist of a firing unit of four guns laid out in a regular or irregular pattern with a predictor or director, a height finder, and power plant centrally located with respect to the guns. The tracks of gun carriages, trailers, and trucks are nearly always visible in an area where a battery has been installed. When the guns are not carefully camouflaged, the outriggers will reveal their positions. The 37-mm gun may be identified by its carriage: which is difficult to conceal. Machine guns are often placed in pits 7 to 10 feet in diameter which furnish a means of identification on an aerial photograph.

SECTION VIII

ANTIMECHANIZED DEFENSE

60. Location.—*a. Active defense.*—The means for protection against mechanized attack are active and passive. The active means include anti-tank guns, smoke, chemicals, artillery, combat aviation, armored vehicles, grenades, and small arms. Usually active and passive means are used in combination, the freedom of maneuver of the enemy mechanized vehicles being limited by the passive means and their destruction accomplished by the active means. Thus, antimechanized weapons may be expected in the vicinity of natural or artificial obstacles or where artificial obstacles would normally be placed. Antitank guns depend upon direct laying fire and therefore must have a good field of fire at ranges up to 1,000 yards. They are often found covering long, straight stretches of road.

b. Passive defense.—Obstacles such as mines, ditches, barricades, and demolitions will be located at tank defiles such as bridges across unfordable streams and roads through heavy woods where it is difficult or impossible for the vehicles to detour. When located on roads, obstacles will generally be placed around curves to obtain the element of surprise. Artificial obstacles will usually be joined with natural obstacles such as lakes, marshes, heavy woods, and rocky ground.

c. Protection of obstacles.—An obstacle is not of full value unless protected by fire. The interpreter should attempt to locate the protecting force.

61. Identification.—The antitank mine is probably the most effective artificial obstacle. Most mines are round, from 7 to 10 inches in diameter, and usually are laid in rows. Unless the mines are carefully buried and covered, these rows or bands of mines generally can be seen on an aerial photograph. When laid from trucks the tracks will often be seen more readily than the mines. Wire rolls or "concertinas" across roads may be seen on aerial photographs of scale 1:2,000 or larger. Most artificial obstacles, such as road blocks and antitank ditches, can be recognized easily on aerial photographs because they present an unnatural pattern or design.

SECTION IX
FIELD ARTILLERY POSITIONS

62. Characteristic positions.—*a. Location.*—A battery of artillery usually consists of four guns spaced in an irregular line at intervals of 25 to 30 yards. Batteries are generally located under some type of cover, either natural or artificial. Positions difficult to locate on aerial photographs are those well concealed in villages, quarries, along roads, thickets, hedges, woods, ditches, or ravines. A good camouflage net, properly garnished and erected, offers artificial cover which is often effective.

b. Identification.—Batteries are usually spotted on aerial photographs from tracks leading to them, by camouflage being too regular in its outline, by piles of ammunition near the position, by blast marks, and by unusual activity in the immediate vicinity of the guns. The guns themselves are only a small part of the evidence of the existence of the battery and are rarely seen on a photograph. Batteries in woods are discovered by slashings in front of the guns, white marks in the woods resulting from disturbances of the surface of the ground and scattering of debris, loops and doubling trails entering woods, and by trucks and prime movers parked near the gun position.

63. Tracks.—*a. Single vehicles.*—Troops are often unaware of the danger invited by leaving tracks, even of single vehicles, in open fields. An interpreter when first viewing a photograph or a stereo pair hastily scans the area for tracks. Many times tracks serve as guiding arrows pointing toward the battery position. Tractors and similar vehicles are the worst offenders of camouflage discipline since their turns are usually deeply cut into the earth.

b. Traffic.—Blotched spots on a photograph often aid the interpreter in locating active positions. These spots are a result of a difference in texture of the ground caused by multiple tracks made by men and vehicles. The locality in which such blotched spots are present will warrant close scrutiny by the interpreter.

[. . .]

66. Wire communication.—Cable lines connect observation posts, artillery batteries, command posts, and headquarters. Their installation may precede that of important establishments, thus giving advance notice of future operations in an area. Cable lines from permanent installations such as coast defense and other large caliber guns are usually buried but may be distinguished by their straight course, angular changes in direction, and fuzzy appearance on aerial photographs. In a mobile situation, lines are laid on top of the ground and are usually inconspicuous, except where they cross roads where, if buried, they may be detected by a dark streak. When in use in active operations, the dark streaks across the roads will disappear, but tracks or paths along the route of the line will appear as the result of men repairing breaks.

[. . .]

Section XI
ENGINEER ACTIVITIES

71. Significance.—A familiarity with the activities of engineers allows predictions as to the possible employment of other enemy troops. In forces the size of corps and larger, engineers employ many types of equipment which, if in the open, is easily identified and the engineer activity is consequently disclosed. Below are listed some of the elements of information peculiar to engineer activities.

Possible enemy line of action	*Engineer activities*
a. Attack.	*a.* (1) Working well forward with road equipment.
	(2) Reinforcement and construction of bridges.
	(3) Construction of mine fields and road blocks on one flank only.
	(4) Construction of advanced landing fields.
	(5) Dumps well forward.
b. Defend.	*b.* (1) Establishing field fortification material dumps well forward.
	(2) Active road construction and maintenance.
	(3) Construction of barriers on both flanks.
	(4) Construction of entrenchments.
	(5) Construction and improvement of landing fields.
	(6) Increased camouflage activity.

c. Withdraw.	*c.* (1) Preparation of barriers and demolitions in zone of withdrawal. (2) Moving heavy engineer equipment to the rear. (3) Slight maintenance of artery roads. (4) Construction of temporary landing fields in rear. (5) Preparation of defensive positions and of barriers and demolitions in rear areas.
d. Delay.	*d.* Engineer activities the same as in a withdrawal, but without preparation of rear defensive positions.

72. Equipment.—Enemy engineer equipment may be expected to parallel our own. The interpreter should therefore be able to recognize various special items of equipment and know their general use. Construction work is usually quite conspicuous when started, but the presence of equipment, as evidence that it is to be started, is often more important to commanders.

73. River crossings.—*a. Importance.*—Intelligence and counter-intelligence are keyed to their highest pitch in river crossings. Aerial photographs are employed extensively by both the attack and defense in this type of operation.

b. Attack.—When our forces are to attack a river line, the location of the enemy's reserves, the routes by which he may bring them forward, and the location of good crossing points are of prime importance. The officer in charge of interpretation may be called upon to furnish a detailed report on the condition of stream banks, locations of points of enemy resistance, extent of cover on both sides of river, possible bridge locations, and other information which would require more than normal photography and interpretation.

c. Defense.—(1) Where a river line is to be defended, photographic studies will be carefully made to determine the logical river crossing points from the location of—

(*a*) Approaches to river.

(*b*) Points along the river where there is moderate current, fairly deep water extending close to both shores, sloping banks, and existing road net nearby.

(*c*) Enemy troop concentrations.

(d) Engineer river crossing equipment concealed in final assembly areas, such as woods near the river.

(e) Old bridge and ferry sites which might be used advantageously as crossing points.

(2) If the location in forward areas of assault boats, footbridge, and ponton bridge equipage can be determined, it will be easier for the commander to estimate the approximate location of the enemy's main effort. Photographs of a ponton bridge already in place are of value as a bombing objective for our air forces and to determine the loads the bridge will carry. A photograph of the beginning of a ponton bridge is of great value to ground forces as proper steps can be taken to oppose its construction and use.

Section XII
ADVANCED LANDING FIELDS

74. Importance.—Advanced landing fields are of all types. They are generally located in or near the theater of operations and are used for grasshopper, observation, photographic, interceptor, and light and medium bombing airplanes. Information concerning the enemy's airfields is obtained from first phase interpretation and turned over immediately to the air force.

75. Construction.—In building advanced landing fields, construction work is kept to a minimum not only because of economy and speed but because it is impossible to conceal construction work while in progress and very hard to camouflage later. Advanced landing fields will have a minimum of facilities. Dispersion is the most important means of protecting personnel and airplanes. Where level land is used to eliminate grading, it is sometimes necessary to install subsurface drainage lines. These can be seen on an aerial photograph taken months, or even years, later. Advanced fields consisting of metal landing strips are successful, particularly when laid on turf requiring very little grading; the camouflage effect is excellent and improves with use. These fields will generally be located where natural overhead cover can be used for concealment of accessories, such as buildings, operating facilities, and airplanes.

[. . .]

Section XIII
CAMOUFLAGE

77. General.—The interpreter must be thoroughly versed in camouflage methods and technique and must study those of the enemy. Our own manuals on camouflage and protective concealment are FM 5-20, TM 5-265, 5-266, and 5-269; these should be studied.

78. Study of own position.—The officer in charge of interpretation may expect to be charged with photographic inspection of his own unit's positions. Camouflage discipline is the responsibility of every commander, and subordinate commanders must be checked. Close cooperation is essential between the interpretation officer and the camouflage officers to see that camouflage is used where needed and is effectively maintained. The original selection of bivouacs and positions is important as utilization of natural concealment as much as possible is essential.

79. Signs of occupation.—Signs of occupation are obvious when an area can be studied on comparative photographs. However, photographs of territory prior to occupation by the enemy are rare. Signs of activity which do not appear to be the normal civilian activity are the primary means of arriving at enemy locations within an area. An attempt to identify every blemish on a photograph with some civilian activity should be made. Trails should be traced to see if they lead to some field under cultivation or other normal place of civilian activity. New appearing roads or trails should be viewed with the utmost suspicion.

80. Dummy installations.—*a. Purpose.*—Care must be exercised in interpretation work to avoid recording dummies as true installations. Dummies have two purposes:

(1) To deceive or confuse visual observers and bombers.

(2) To deceive interpreters.

The former are hurried jobs and become apparent on photographs. The latter are deliberate, carefully planned and executed.

b. Identification.—Dummy installations frequently may be identified because of the tendency of installers to make the subject too obvious. Exposing characteristics of dummy installations are the following:

(1) White is too white.

(2) Signs of activity inherent to construction of a real installation are lacking.

(3) Size of object or installation smaller than real object.

(4) Installations made by designs on earth (roads and runways) are usually too angular and edges are too well defined.

(5) Objects designed to have depth are more often the opposite of (4) above and have wavy edges.

(6) Lack of shadows, or shadows in the wrong relation to actual objects.

(7) Location not logical for real object.

(8) Absence of communication to object, which would be in evidence on a real object.

(9) Absence of allied or supporting objects. This is a case where a dummy airfield lacks signs of personnel living in the vicinity or where dummy artillery positions have no signs of prime movers and communication.

(10) Lack of maintenance. This is easily determined by comparative photographs.

U.S. Strategic Bombing Survey

A primary activity of Allied aerial reconnaissance was to assess the effects of the strategic bombing campaigns on their intended targets. On November 3, 1944, Secretary of War Henry Stimson formed a survey team to assess the effects of the bombing campaign on Germany, later expanded to include the campaign against Japan. Its brief was, according to the Foreword of the later Summary Report for the Pacific War, "for the purpose of conducting an impartial and expert study of the effects of our aerial attack on Germany, to be used in connection with air attacks on Japan and to establish a basis for evaluating air power as an instrument of military strategy, for planning the future development of the United States armed forces, and for determining future economic policies with respect to the national defense." Notably, and at times controversially, the survey team mostly consisted of civilian specialists. They had access to a plethora of intelligence documents and sources in their work. The final European report, known as the United States Strategic

Bombing Survey (USSBS), was not published until September 30, 1945, and the report on the bombing of Japan came in July 1946. The latter naturally included insights into the destruction delivered of the two atomic bombs delivered on Hiroshima and Nagasaki on August 6 and 9, 1945, respectively. Here is a passage explaining some of the generalized effects:

The Effects of the Atomic Bombs

On 6 August and 9 August 1945, the first two atomic bombs to be used for military purposes were dropped on Hiroshima and Nagasaki respectively. One hundred thousand people were killed, 6 square miles or over 50 percent of the built-up areas of the two cities were destroyed. The first and crucial question about the atomic bomb thus was answered practically and conclusively; atomic energy had been mastered for military purposes and the overwhelming scale of its possibilities had been demonstrated. A detailed examination of the physical, economic, and morale effects of the atomic bombs occupied the attention of a major portion of the Survey's staff in Japan in order to arrive at a more precise definition of the present capabilities and limitations of this radically new weapon of destruction.

Eyewitness accounts of the explosion all describe similar pictures. The bombs exploded with a tremendous flash of blue-white light, like a giant magnesium flare. The flash was of short duration and accompanied by intense glare and heat. It was followed by a tremendous pressure wave and the rumbling sound of the explosion. This sound is not clearly recollected by those who survived near the center of the explosion, although it was clearly heard by others as much as fifteen miles sway. A huge snow-white cloud shot rapidly into the sky and the scene on the ground was obscured first by a bluish haze and then by a purple-brown cloud of dust and smoke.

Such eyewitness accounts reveal the sequence of events. At the time of the explosion, energy was given off in the forms of light, heat, radiation, and pressure. The complete band of radiations, from X- and gamma-rays, through ultraviolet and light rays to the radiant heat of infra-red rays, travelled with the speed of light. The shock wave created by the enormous pressures built up almost instantaneously at the point of explosion but moved out more slowly, that is at about the speed of sound. The superheated gases constituting the original fire ball expanded outward and upward at a slower rate.

The light and radiant heat rays accompanying the flash travelled in a straight line and any opaque object, even a single leaf of a vine, shielded objects lying behind it. The duration of the flash was only a fraction of a second, but it was sufficiently intense to cause third degree burns to exposed human skin up to a distance of a mile. Clothing ignited, though it could be quickly beaten out, telephone poles charred, thatch-roofed houses caught fire. Black or other dark-colored surfaces of combustible material absorbed the heat and immediately charred or burst into flames; white or light-colored surfaces reflected a substantial portion of the rays and were not consumed. Heavy black clay tiles which are an almost universal feature of the roofs of Japanese houses bubbled at distances up to a mile. Test of samples of this tile by the National Bureau of Standards in Washington indicates that temperatures in excess of 1,800° C. must have been generated in the surface of the tile to produce such an effect. The surfaces of granite blocks exposed to the flash scarred and spalled at distances up to almost a mile. In the immediate area of ground zero (the point on the ground immediately below the explosion), the heat charred corpses beyond recognition.

Penetrating rays such as gamma-rays exposed X-ray films stored in the basement of a concrete hospital almost a mile from ground zero. Symptoms of their effect on human beings close to the center of the explosion, who survived other effects thereof, were generally delayed for two or three days. The bone marrow and as a result the process of blood formation were affected. The white corpuscle count went down and the human processes of resisting infection were destroyed. Death generally followed shortly thereafter.

The majority of radiation cases who were at greater distances did not show severe symptoms until 1 to 4 weeks after the explosion. The first symptoms were loss of appetite, lassitude and general discomfort. Within 12 to 48 hours, fever became evident in many cases, going as high as 104° to 105° F., which in fatal cases continued until death. If the fever subsided, the patient usually showed a rapid disappearance of other symptoms and soon regained his feeling of good health. Other symptoms were loss of white blood corpuscles, loss of hair, and decrease in sperm count.

Even though rays of this nature have great powers of penetration, intervening substances filter out portions of them. As the weight of the intervening material increases the percentage of the rays penetrating goes down. It appears that a few feet of concrete, or a somewhat greater thickness of earth, furnished sufficient protection to humans, even those close to ground zero, to prevent serious after effects from radiation.

The blast wave which followed the flash was of sufficient force to press in the roofs of reinforced concrete structures and to flatten completely all less sturdy structures. Due to the height of the explosion, the peak pressure of the wave at ground zero was no higher than that produced by a near miss of a high-explosive bomb, and decreased at greater distances from ground zero. Reflection and shielding by intervening hills and structures produced some unevenness in the pattern. The blast wave, however, was of far greater extent and duration than that of a high-explosive bomb and most reinforced-concrete structures suffered structural damage or collapse up to 700 feet at Hiroshima and 2,000 feet at Nagasaki. Brick buildings were flattened up to 7,300 feet at Hiroshima and 8,500 feet at Nagasaki. Typical Japanese houses of wood construction suffered total collapse up to approximately 7,300 feet at Hiroshima and 8,200 feet at Nagasaki. Beyond these distances structures received less serious damage to roofs, wall partitions, and the like. Glass windows were blown out at distances up to 5 miles. The blast wave, being of longer duration than that caused by high-explosive detonations, was accompanied by more flying debris. Window frames, doors, and partitions which would have been shaken down by a near-miss of a high-explosive bomb were hurled at high velocity through those buildings which did not collapse. Machine tools and most other production equipment in industrial plants were not directly damaged by the blast wave, but were damaged by collapsing buildings or ensuing general fires.

The above description mentions all the categories of the destructive action by the atomic-bomb explosions at Hiroshima and Nagasaki. There were no other types of action. Nothing was vaporized or disintegrated; vegetation is growing again immediately under the center of the explosions; there are no indications that radio-activity continued after the explosion to a sufficient degree to harm human beings.

★★★

One of the main purposes of aerial reconnaissance was to provide information for the production of military maps (the other key purpose was damage assessment). During World War II, military maps were time-critical documents. They had to show the most accurate plotting of roads, tracks, rail lines, significant buildings, bridges, waterways, topography, and dozens of other elements, but might also include up-to-date information about both friendly and enemy deployments (depending on the sensitivity and distribution of the map), ideally presented to frontline commanders within hours of the aerial photographs being taken. The U.S. intelligence services drew heavily upon the skills of the Army Map Service (AMS), which was founded in 1941 for the purposes of publishing and distributing military topographic maps across the U.S. armed services. The cartographic output of this branch, which operated under the umbrella of the Corps of Engineers, was massive—during World War II, the AMS produced an estimated 500 million topographic maps, including 70 million copies of nearly 3,000 different maps for the Normandy invasion in June 1944. The following intelligence manual, Military Maps (1940), explains the different types of military map and also the expediencies that might be required to turn reconnaissance photographs into useful 2D visualizations of the battlefield.

★★★

From FM 30-20, *Basic Field Manual, Military Intelligence: Military Maps* (1940)

SECTION VII
MILITARY MAPS AND AERIAL PHOTOGRAPHS

■ 30. MAP CLASSIFICATION.—*a. General.*—The maps used in a theater of operations will consist of those available at the outbreak of hostilities and of those produced thereafter. The availability of maps will depend largely upon the location of the theater of operations and will vary from crude small scale planimetric maps to accurate well-prepared topographic maps suitable for enlargement. They will include various special purpose maps, such as road maps, railroad maps, aeronautical charts, etc. Large scale topographic maps suitable for tactical operations of small units may be expected only in isolated areas of limited size. Except in certain parts of Western Europe, topographic maps at scales as large as 1:20,000 will not be found.

b. Types of maps.—Maps for use in a theater of operations naturally fall into classification according to scale. The use of the various types of maps will depend upon the character of the theater of operations, type of operations, and nature of the opposition encountered.

(1) *Small scale maps.*—Maps of small scale varying from 1:1,000,000 to 1:7,000,000 are intended for the general planning and strategical studies of the commanders of larger units. Various general maps have been designed for these purposes.

(2) *Intermediate scale maps.*—Maps of intermediate scale, normally from 1:200,000 to 1:500,000, are intended for planning strategic operations,

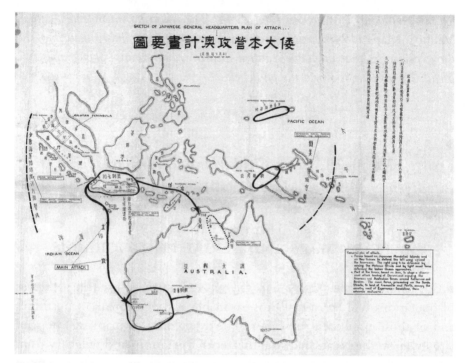

Assessing enemy mapwork required caution and skepticism. This Japanese map was actually a fake plan for an invasion of Australia in 1942. (Australian Department of Defence)

including the movement, concentration, and supply of troops. The Strategic Map of the United States, 1: 500,000, has been designed for these purposes.

(3) *Medium scale maps.*—Maps of medium scale, normally from 1:50,000 to 1:125,000, are intended for strategical, tactical, and administrative studies by units ranging in size from the corps to the regiment. The United States Geological Survey map, scale 1:62,500, with wooded areas and road classifications added, has been found suitable for these purposes.

For strategic areas, the War Department produces maps of this type. While not suitable for all purposes, the scale of 1:62,500 has been found to be the most advantageous for recording topographical detail for future use. For campaign, maps of this scale can be used for the purpose intended or may be enlarged or reduced according to the existing needs.

(4) *Large scale maps.*—Maps of large scale, normally not greater than 1:20,000, are intended for the technical and tactical battle needs of the Field Artillery and of the Infantry. It is unlikely that maps of this category will be found to cover extensive areas. The battle map scale 1:20,000 has been designed for this purpose.

c. Preparation of various types.—Suitable topographic maps prepared during peace will be utilized when available. When not existent at the outbreak of hostilities, maps of the various types must be promptly prepared. These maps will consist of those prepared initially by compiling information from existing source material and those produced by troops in the field.

(1) The small scale general map will be compiled from source material and reproduced as promptly as possible. This work is appropriate for base plants.

(2) The intermediate scale strategic map must be compiled from source material. This compilation will be done in base plants or by GHQ topographic battalions.

(3) In an unmapped theater, data will rarely exist which will permit compilation of medium scale maps. The medium scale map, when not existent and when its use is essential, must be prepared by troops in the field. Topographic battalions can prepare maps at this scale. However, for maximum map production, the effort of the topographic battalions should be confined initially to maps of one scale. As the large scale map is normally of greater immediate importance to units in contact, preparation of the large scale map will normally have priority. Under these conditions and from the data thus secured, the medium scale map will be compiled later by the GHQ and army topographic battalions.

(4) The large scale maps, when available, will normally have the widest distribution in combat. For limited areas, data secured for maps of the medium scale will be suitable for enlargement in preparation of the large scale map. In general, large scale maps must be prepared by troops in the field for the area of immediate operation. Two general types of large scale maps, normally at a scale of 1:20,000, will be furnished, depending upon the situation but primarily upon the time available.

(*a*) The large scale map initially furnished in mobile situations, in development phases, and in all other situations where time is limited to a period of hours or days, will normally consist of a map substitute; it may either be in the form of direct reproductions of wide coverage photographs or mosaics, or in the form of the provisional map, with or without relief, prepared from such photographs. This hasty type of map will be required primarily by lower echelons, including the corps when operating as part of an army. In mobile situations, the holding attack of an army, which initially would require maps only to a limited depth, may frequently be provided only with map substitutes.

(*b*) The battle map will replace all map substitutes in the area of immediate operations as the situation becomes more stabilized. [The manual defines the battle map as: "A map, prepared normally by photogrammetric means and at a scale of 1:20,000, which is suitable for the tactical and technical needs of all arms."] It may subsequently be used for the preparation of the medium scale map.

d. Aeronautical charts.—Sectional aeronautical charts, scale 1:500,000, and regional aeronautical charts, scale 1:1,000,000 published by the United States Coast and Geodetic Survey, give complete coverage of the United States for air navigation. Other forms of aeronautical charts for specialized use are also available. The aeronautical chart consists of a map upon which information pertaining to air navigation has been added, and its primary use is for aerial navigation. Aeronautical charts covering many important areas of the earth's surface at various scales are readily obtainable. If not available in event of hostilities, they will be compiled at the earliest practicable opportunity.

e. Aerial photographs.—The aerial photograph read directly or stereoscopically is particularly suited for minor tactics, and for supplying detailed information of terrain in limited areas. Photographs will generally be of a scale of 1:20,000 or larger. Urgent needs for special tactical, technical, or intelligence purposes may be met by the production of contact prints within the airplane after day or night photography.

★★★

Ship identification was the bread-and-butter task of naval intelligence officers. The naval intelligence publication ONI 223, Ship Shapes: Anatomy and

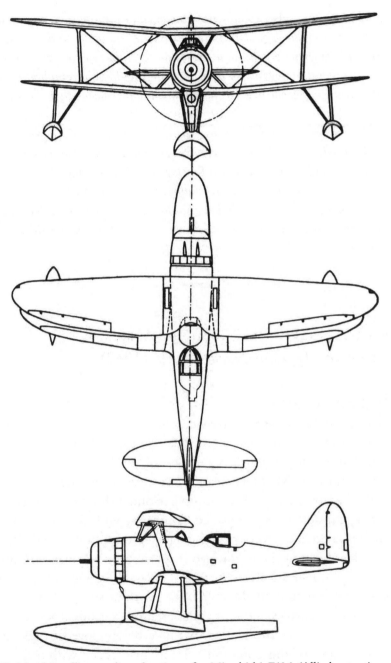

A U.S. Naval Intelligence line drawing of a Mitsubishi F1M (Allied reporting name "Pete"), a Japanese reconnaissance floatplane. (Office of Naval Intelligence)

Types of Naval Vessels *explains the fundamental principles of ship anatomy, giving the observer the logical tools to rationalize the vessel and thus identify sufficient unique characteristics so as to define the ship type or even the specific ship. As the manual suggests, ship identification could be a complicated matter. The unprecedented global burst of naval shipbuilding meant that the seas were awash with literally thousands of different vessels, but belonging to common types (destroyers, frigates, battleships, carriers, etc.), the fine-grade distinctions between each of them only discernible to those with a specialist's eye for differences in mast configuration, gun positions, superstructure layout, or a thousand other details. The key, as with much intelligence interpretation, was to start with the big category distinctions and then slowly work down to the finer details, comparing what you saw with silhouettes, line drawings, and photographs of individual ships in other naval manuals.*

★★★

From U.S. Navy, ONI 223, *Ship Shapes: Anatomy and Types of Naval Vessels* (1942)

INTRODUCTION

Combatants in the present war have consistently bombed and shot at their own ships and those of their allies. A large body of opinion maintains that the Italians, for instance, would be obliging enough to eliminate their fleet from the Mediterranean if left to their own devices.

While the objective of all seagoing personnel should be to recognize important ships or types at a glance, familiarity with the details of naval design illustrated in the following pages may prove of value to the student of ship identification. Determination of a ship's type must constitute a primary step in identification in combat areas. Since accurate estimation of a ship's size is extremely difficult at sea, an observer may have occasion to resort to certain rules of thumb to differentiate various types of fighting ships. A discussion of the factors that may be employed to distinguish these types, and of the common variants that occur within the types themselves, will be found in this section of O.N.I. 223.

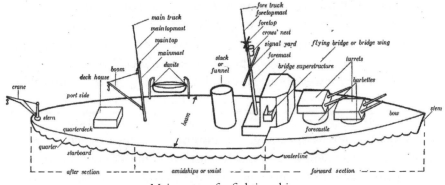

Main parts of a fighting ship.

Of all fighting ships, the old Monitor must have been about the easiest to identify. She had a single turret and a single stack on a wide flat hull, and that was all that could be said about her. Modern warships have become a good deal more complex. In fact there are very few warships in the world that look precisely alike. An expert can tell even sister ships apart by minor differences in their masts or superstructures. All ships share in some degree the essential characteristics of their type, and as one becomes familiar with ships one also becomes increasingly aware of the peculiar national character that distinguishes ships of the world's navies.

"Spot" identification of ships at sea is not always possible. The appearance of individual warships is constantly undergoing alteration in time of war and consideration must be given, for purposes of identification, to elements of structure that are least subject to change, such as main armament and hull proportions. "Progressive" identification, or identification through observation of detail, will often constitute the basis for a more dependable check on a ship's identity than the general impression of an observer. For this reason, variations in structural elements that appear in all fighting ships are illustrated in this section, as well as those which serve to differentiate types, with terms commonly applied to them. The progressive method is considered especially well suited to descriptive reporting of ships' appearance. A method of reporting such data appears in O.N.I. 223- K, *Warships in Code*, recently published by the Division of Naval Intelligence.

[. . .]

The student of ship identification should first of all familiarize himself with the types of ship that make up a modern fleet. [. . .] Each of these ships has been designed to play an aggressive role in combat. Each has its place and function in the disposition of the Fleet when at sea. Not all of these ships, however, are intended solely for operation with others. A cruiser or lighter vessel may execute an independent combat mission, preying upon commerce or clearing the sea of raiders and other enemy naval units. Generally speaking, the number of ships of each type in a well-balanced navy will vary inversely with size. Thus, for every battleship, approximately two heavy cruisers, two light cruisers and five destroyers will be built. The relative proportion of our existing carriers or of carriers building or contemplated cannot be expressed in similar terms and is therefore omitted. It will suffice to say that the proportion of ships of this type in our Navy will be greatly increased over the pre-war level.

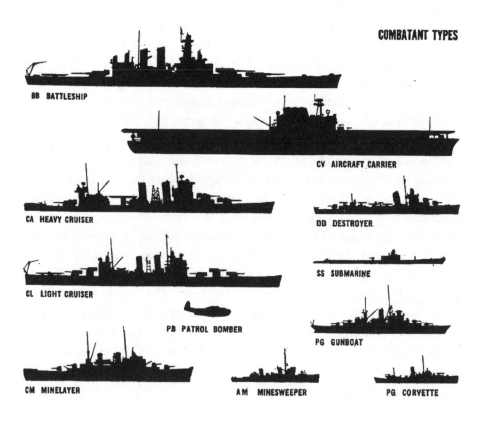

COMBATANT TYPES

BB BATTLESHIP

CV AIRCRAFT CARRIER

CA HEAVY CRUISER

DD DESTROYER

CL LIGHT CRUISER

SS SUBMARINE

PB PATROL BOMBER

PG GUNBOAT

CM MINELAYER

AM MINESWEEPER

PG CORVETTE

For every ship that is built to meet an opponent in battle, a dozen are built to perform prosaic but necessary jobs for the maintenance, supply, and protection of the Fleet and its shore establishments. Many types of repair, supply and transport vessels are constantly engaged in serving and maintaining our two-ocean fleet. Extended naval operations would often be impossible without these ships. In waters where adequate docking, repair and fuel facilities do not exist, the crippling of an enemy repair ship or oiler may require modification or abandonment of an important operation. The destruction of an enemy's auxiliaries must, therefore, be regarded as an objective of major importance.

Identification of such units is important. An observer must be able to distinguish enemy ships of these types from corresponding vessels of his own navy and of his allies'. Accurate reporting of minor enemy ship types present in an operating area is an important factor in anticipating

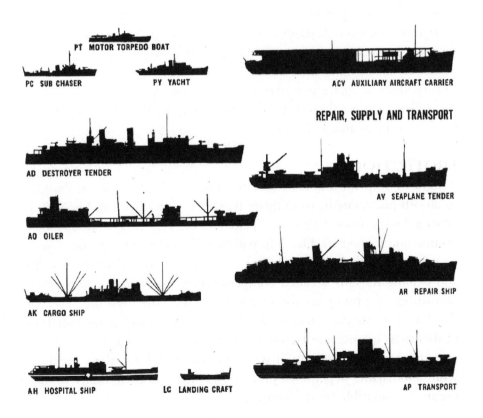

PT MOTOR TORPEDO BOAT

PC SUB CHASER

PY YACHT

ACV AUXILIARY AIRCRAFT CARRIER

REPAIR, SUPPLY AND TRANSPORT

AD DESTROYER TENDER

AV SEAPLANE TENDER

AO OILER

AR REPAIR SHIP

AK CARGO SHIP

AH HOSPITAL SHIP

LC LANDING CRAFT

AP TRANSPORT

an opponent's plans and in the formation of strategic as well as tactical decisions. It is not enough, therefore, simply to know your own and the enemy's major combatant ships. Fliers especially should become familiar with such minor vessels in order to report accurately the types of the many ships that will be observed in theaters of war.

A ship, to be classed as a *fighting ship*, must be capable of inflicting damage and of sustaining or avoiding damage. She must possess sufficient speed and maneuverability to execute her mission and the capacity to proceed independently to a scene of action. The type of a warship is determined by the degree to which each of these qualities has been stressed in her design.

ARMAMENT

Capacity to "dish it out" is a primary attribute of fighting ships. Ships may be designed to inflict damage by *shells* from their guns, *torpedoes* from their tubes, *bombs* from aircraft they may carry, or by *depth charges* or *mines*. Battleships and cruisers are essentially *gun* ships, although they carry other weapons. Carriers, minelayers and torpedo boats are designed for special attack functions, with guns provided largely for defense, while destroyers and submarines are dual armament ships, using either guns or torpedoes. Larger types carry secondary batteries, primarily intended for defense against destroyers or submarines, or, if "dual purpose," for protection from attack from the air.

PROTECTION

A fighting ship must also be able to "take it." A ship may be designed to absorb punishment, to mitigate its effect, or to avoid it. She may be provided with *armor*: heavy steel plate around vital parts to defeat shells, bombs, and torpedoes. Her hull will be subdivided into separate spaces, or provided with bulges or blisters, to confine the effects of flooding and explosion. This is called compartmentation. *Damage control systems* consisting of provisions for counterflooding, fire fighting, etc., are developed in varying degree in all types. Speed and maneuverability in themselves constitute factors of protection in smaller types in which armament and protection, have been sacrificed for these qualities, while submarines depend for protection largely on their ability to make themselves invisible by submerging.

MOBILITY

Most fighting ships are propelled by high-pressure steam boilers and geared turbine engines, although diesel or reciprocating engines are sometimes used in smaller types. Diesels are used in submarines when operating on the surface, electric storage battery motors when submerged.

Since a large proportion of total displacement and space is allotted to armament and protection in the design of battleships, these ships do not attain the high speeds of many smaller combat units. Carriers are designed for speed, with corresponding sacrifice of armor. Cruisers' speed will range from 30 knots, which will permit a heavy cruiser to operate with the fleet and outrun most battleships, to speeds of over 40 knots in lighter types. Speed is essential to a destroyer's functions and new types are capable of attaining or bettering that of any cruiser.

SEA KEEPING

Without the capacity to reach a scene of operations, execute a mission, and return to a base, even the fastest and most powerful fighting ship would be of little value.

To bring an enemy to action is the battleship's primary function, and these ships must carry crews and provisions necessary to take them into battle with enough shells and fuel and food aboard to permit them to fight and return. Since cruisers are often required to perform independent missions at great distances, sea keeping capacity is a vital consideration in their design. Carriers must also be designed to accommodate provision for extended operations and fuel for their aircraft. Destroyers, as they often operate with battle fleets or in convoy, must also carry provision for such work, subject to limitations of size, while submarines are required to remain in enemy waters for extended periods. It will, therefore, be seen that sea keeping is a very important factor in the design of all more important types of fighting ships.

The bulky hull of the battleship reflects capacity to accommodate provision for sea repair and for storage of immense quantities of fuel, water, food, ships stores, and lubricating oil, while the proportions of destroyer hulls indicate limitations in sea-keeping capacity inherent in their type.

[. . .]

DECK LINES AND SUPERSTRUCTURE TYPES

Breaks in deck lines will often differentiate one ship from another. These are not usually difficult to observe in more modern ships, but may not be clearly distinguishable in older battleships which carry their secondary batteries along their sides rather than on deck.

A ship's superstructure may fall into one of three classifications. When a structure occurs forward of the ship's center she is known as a "single island" type. If two unconnected deck structures appear the ship is a "twin island" type, while if the ship has a continuous structure amidships she is of the "center island" type. Further classifications result from a combination of deck lines and superstructures. It should be remembered that it is often difficult to classify positively superstructure types which appear in many larger ships because of the presence of boats and other gear which clutter the midship sections of these ships and often obscure their superstructures. Narrow "wells" or spaces between superstructure elements are also difficult to observe from any position other than full broadside. (In this connection see *Tirpitz*). It is therefore well to avoid reporting a ship as having any special type of superstructure unless one has had an opportunity for thorough observation from a broadside position.

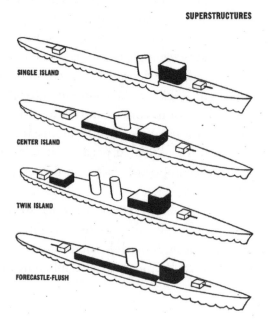

SUPERSTRUCTURES

SINGLE ISLAND

CENTER ISLAND

TWIN ISLAND

FORECASTLE-FLUSH

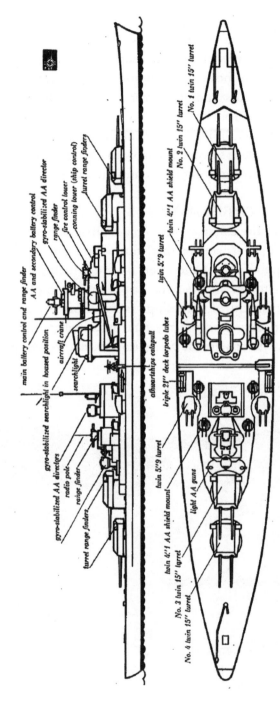

Tirpitz is the latest example of German capital ship design. Unusual beam makes for great stability and permits extensive compartmentation. Speed, underwater protection, and endurance take precedence over gun power and armor. *Tirpitz* is a ship better designed for ocean raiding than for fleet action.

ARMAMENT

Gun houses, like turrets, are wholly enclosed. Turrets generally occur along the centerlines of larger ships. They are of greater size and their proportions are lower than those of gun houses. A great variety of main armament dispositions occurs among the world's fighting ships. These are usually clearly discernible from the air and their observation constitutes one of the most useful determinants in identification. Since secondary armament is often difficult to see it is advisable to base identification only on main armament appearing along the centerline of the ship observed.

SHIPS' GUNS AND THEIR MOUNTS

With the exception of the casemate gun (generally a secondary gun on older ships) the types [of armament that] form the main armament of all combatant ships [range from] the open mount armament of lighter craft and submarines to the heavy twin, triple or quadruple turret of battleships. Main armament of battleships ranges from 16in. down to 11in. guns. Heavy cruisers usually carry 8in. guns, light cruisers 6.1in. to 4.5in. guns. Destroyer armament varies from 5.5in. to 3in. guns.

A U.S. Naval Intelligence photograph of a Japanese *Fuso*-class battleship, the photo taken in 1937. (National Museum of the U.S. Navy)

MASTS

Masts cannot always be assigned to one or another of the several types. Some are "border-line" cases, falling between two types, others are unique structures which belong in none of the standard classifications. Generally speaking, however, masts may be classified under one of the types which appear on these pages. It should be remembered that, of all elements of a ship's structure, masts are most subject to alteration and addition. An example of this may be seen in older Japanese battleships, which began with tripod or other multiple masts which have by now become so cluttered with galleries and flying bridges that the basic supporting structure has become invisible. These masts now fall into the category of pagodas or towers, but in their transitional phases it was impossible to assign them to any definite classification. Masts must, therefore, be observed carefully but in many instances should not be used as the basis for positive identification of a given ship. For identification purposes, masts must often be considered in relation to bridge structures. Here again it is often unwise to assign a combination of mast and bridge to a definite classification where doubt exists in the observer's mind. Bridge forms may vary from low, boxlike structures to high towers. Typical tower bridges appear in *Rodney* and *Nelson*, and in our own *New Mexico*, and may be distinguished from tower or pagoda masts by the fact that the bridge structure rises vertically from the main deck, without a secondary structure at the base. Certain types of mast-bridge assemblies are characteristic of various nationalities. The pylon–high bridge combination is typically Japanese, while the bridge-tower combination is common in large German ships.

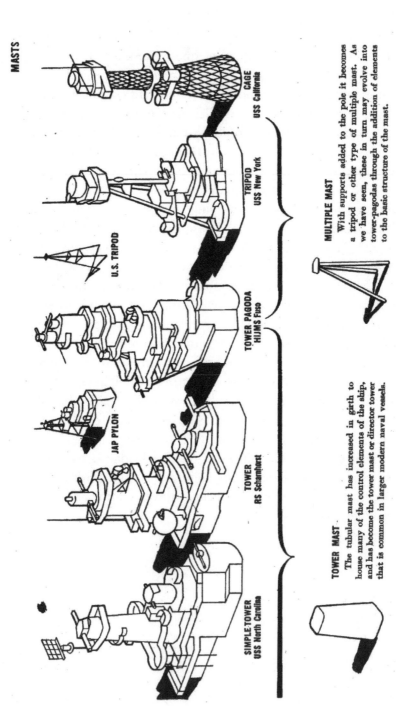

MASTS

SIMPLE TOWER
USS North Carolina

TOWER
RS Scharnhorst

JAP PYLON

TOWER PAGODA
HIJMS Fuso

U.S. TRIPOD

TRIPOD
USS New York

CAGE
USS California

TOWER MAST.

The tubular mast has increased in girth to house many of the control elements of the ship, and has become the tower mast or director tower that is common in larger modern naval vessels.

MULTIPLE MAST.

With supports added to the pole it becomes a tripod or other type of multiple mast. As we have seen, these in turn may evolve into tower-pagodas through the addition of elements to the basic structure of the mast.

CHAPTER 5

Secret Intelligence
and Counterintelligence

Our first manual in this chapter comes from the archives of what was one of the defining secret intelligence services of both World War II and indeed of the 20th century in general, an organization that broke the mold of previous visions of what U.S. intelligence was and could be. The Office of Strategic Services (OSS) began its life on July 11, 1941, when President Franklin D. Roosevelt appointed William J. Donovan to head a new government office, the Coordinator of Information (COI). The COI would report directly to the White House and was charged mainly with collecting and analyzing national security data, and distributing that data throughout key corridors of government. Once war had started, however, the ambitious Donovan pushed to have the COI moved under the military umbrella of the Joint Chiefs of Staff (JCS), and on June 13, 1942, the COI became the Office of Strategic Services.

The OSS was a true covert operations group, its personnel trained in the dark arts of espionage, sabotage, psychological warfare, but above all, intelligence-gathering. It specialized in putting agents behind enemy lines, even deep into the Axis nations themselves, training both Americans and foreign citizens to set up effective and extensive spy networks. In total, the OSS also established more than 40 overseas offices.

The OSS operatives showed bravery and innovation, but their efforts were not always appreciated by senior military and governmental figures. Hostility from MacArthur, as noted in our introduction, kept them out of the South West Pacific Area (SWPA), while domestic antipathy from J. Edgar Hoover of the Federal Bureau of Investigation (FBI) and Nelson Rockefeller, the Coordinator of Inter-American Affairs, alienated the OSS from the Americas. Thus, they

Major General William J. "Wild Bill" Donovan (left), the director of the OSS, is here seen with intelligence officer Colonel William Harding Jackson c. 1945. (U.S. Army Signal Corps)

directed most of their efforts towards Europe, East Asia, and Africa. The OSS was disbanded by the end of September 1945, its activities subsequently taken over by its successors, the Department of State's Bureau of Intelligence and Research (INR) and the Central Intelligence Agency (CIA).

★★★

From *Secret Intelligence Field Manual: Strategic Services (Provisional)* (1944)

3. FUNCTIONS OF THE SECRET INTELLIGENCE BRANCH
    a. The principal function of the Secret Intelligence Branch is to collect and evaluate secret intelligence and to disseminate such intelligence to appropriate branches of OSS and to military and other authorized agencies. Supplementary functions are: to establish and maintain direct liaison with Allied secret intelligence agencies; and

to obtain information from underground groups by direct contact or other means.

(1) *Collection of information*

Information is collected in neutral, enemy, and enemy-occupied countries, outside of the Western Hemisphere, by secret intelligence operatives and agents working under cover. This information is obtained by personal observation, through strategically placed informants, or by other means available. Information is also collected in Allied countries through contact with Allied secret intelligence agencies and representatives of underground or other groups and from individuals who have special knowledge.

(2) *Evaluation of information*

(a) Information is evaluated both as to the reliability of the source and as to the truth, credibility, or probability of the information itself. The following rating scale is used in evaluating the source:

> A—Completely reliable
> B—Usually reliable
> C—Fairly reliable
> D—Not usually reliable
> E—Unreliable
> F—Untried

(b) The following rating scale is used in evaluating the truth, credibility, or probability of the information:
> 1—Report confirmed by other sources
> 2—Probably true
> 3—Possibly true
> 4—Doubtful
> 5—Improbable
> 0—Truth cannot be judged

Thus a report rated A-2 would be a probably true report coming from a completely reliable source.

(c) In Washington, the responsibility for the evaluation of information is lodged in the SI Reporting Board. In the field, Reports Officers perform this function. So far as the evaluation of the *source* of material is concerned, the field offices and the desk heads, through the maintenance of records on operatives and agents, are able to furnish the reporting officials with information from which reasonable conclusions may be drawn. As to the presumptive reliability of the *content* of reports, the operatives and the field offices contribute their opinion, the geographic desk heads add whatever comment they may be in a position to make, and the reporting officials check the information against their own records and knowledge and against information available in other branches of OSS, particularly R&A, or in other government agencies.

(3) *Dissemination of intelligence*

(a) SI disseminates intelligence to the other branches of OSS, and selected intelligence to the Military Intelligence Division (MID), the Office of Naval Intelligence (ONI), Air Intelligence (A-2), Joint Intelligence Committee, the State Department, other authorized U. S. government agencies, and to the designated authorities of Allied governments.

(b) Secret intelligence is also disseminated from field bases either directly by the Reports Officer or through the Joint Intelligence Collection Agencies (JICA) in the Theaters of Operations where such agencies have been established.

(c) Dissemination of secret intelligence is the function of the Reports Officer at an OSS field base and of the SI Reporting Board at Washington. The SI desk heads may suggest the dissemination to be given a report.

(d) In general, operatives should not attempt to disseminate intelligence within the actual area of operations, both for reasons of security and for lack of ability properly to evaluate.

[. . .]

An underwater combat swimmer from the OSS Detachment 404 Maritime Unit recovers consciousness after suffering a malfunction with rebreathing apparatus in 1944. (USG)

SECTION V—METHODS OF OPERATIONS

14. *GENERAL*

OSS is authorized to conduct secret intelligence activities in all areas, exclusive of the Western Hemisphere. In neutral areas, however, SI activities may be limited by understandings with the chiefs of diplomatic missions.

15. *SECURITY*

a. Security is the *sine qua non* of secret intelligence activities. If security is lacking anywhere in the process of collecting and disseminating information, the continued functioning of an individual or of an entire network is endangered.

b. The factor of security is present to a greater or lesser degree in every phase of secret intelligence activities; however, several general principles governing security may be stated:

(1) No one in a secret intelligence organization should be told more than he has to know to do his own job. The less any one man knows, the less he can let slip—or be forced to tell—if taken by the enemy. As far as possible, the different activities carried on by an intelligence organization should be boxed in water-tight compartments.

(2) Secret intelligence personnel should be suspicious of every individual until his loyalty has been proven beyond a doubt.

(3) Secret intelligence personnel should proceed on the assumption that all telephones are tapped, all mail censored, all rooms wired, all radio messages read by the enemy.

c. Following are some of the specific security measures that may be taken in the field:

(1) Cutouts should be used by the operative whenever he considers it unsafe to come into direct contact with another individual.

(2) Meeting places should be selected for the opportunities they afford the participants for an inconspicuous encounter.

(3) Danger signals should be arranged in advance of meetings. In order to avoid detection at the time of signaling, a system should be used whereby a pre-determined signal is given only when it is desired to indicate the absence of danger. If danger is present, no signal will be given.

(4) Recognition signals to be used between persons meeting for the first time should also be arranged in advance.

16. COVER

a. Every SI operative and agent working in enemy, enemy-occupied or neutral territory must have a suitable cover—that is, an ostensibly legitimate reason for being where he is.

b. Obviously, cover must be safe. That is, it must successfully shield the operative's secret activities. In the second place, it must allow the operative sufficient freedom of action to perform his mission. For the

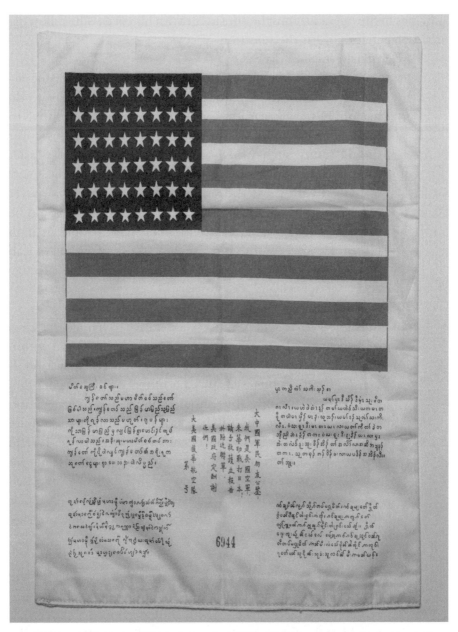

A silk "blood chit" issued for use by the Office of Strategic Services in the China-Burma-India Theater. Written in several native languages, it reads, "This foreign person (American) has come to China to help the war effort. Soldiers and civilians, one and all, should save and protect him." (CIA)

activities of the operative must be consistent with his cover. The following broad principles govern the selection of cover:

(1) *Social freedom*

A good cover will permit the operative to mingle inconspicuously with the kind of people he will have to see to do his job. His particular mission might require the operative to meet people of all levels of society, in which case his cover should justify such varied association. It is generally easier for a man to associate with those beneath him in the social scale than with those above him. Thus, a doctor or a lawyer can legitimately meet all kinds of people, while it would be suspicious for a stevedore to associate with people in high places. However, some jobs, such as those of waiter or cab driver, allow considerable social freedom and provide effective cover for agents.

(2) *Financial freedom*

A good cover will permit the operative to handle the sums of money his SI activities will require, for he must live within the limits of the income received from his cover occupation. If he is to handle substantial amounts of money and to entertain a good deal, the operative should adopt a cover occupation that pays well. On the other hand, if circumstances require him to adopt a poorly-paid occupation, he must be careful not to spend more money than the income from such an occupation would normally allow. Many covers are wrecked on the rock of finances. Unusual bank deposits or irregular financial transactions are prime causes of counter-espionage investigations.

(3) *Freedom of movement*

A good cover will permit the operative to travel to the extent necessitated by his mission. If his particular mission requires extensive traveling, he should choose a cover that would make frequent journeys perfectly natural. It must be remembered, however, that every trip made must have its particular cover story—a story consistent either with the operative's assumed occupation or with his assumed personal life. This story should be prepared in advance and be as true as circumstances permit.

(4) *Freedom of leisure*

A good cover will allow the operative sufficient leisure time for the conduct of his SI activities. Therefore his cover occupation must not demand too much of his time. If possible, the cover chosen should permit short or irregular hours of work.

c. In the selection of cover, an occupation should be chosen with which the operative is familiar and which is consistent with his own experience. He should draw as much from his own life as is safe to do. Thus his story will be better able to stand investigation. The most effective cover is that which is as near truth as possible. In any case, the cover selected will be limited by the operative's personal characteristics and abilities, as well as by his mission.

d. Where the cover is almost, or wholly, artificial, the operative must take every precaution to live the part. His dress, appearance, personal effects, speech, mannerisms, and every action must conform. He must be sure that nothing he wears, possesses, says, or does will make him conspicuous or reveal that he is not what he pretends to be.

e. Cover is so important, and good covers so rare, that in many cases the finding of a good cover will determine the selection of the operative and the definition of his mission.

f. The selection of a suitable cover is the responsibility of the section chief or desk head. Arrangements with organizations outside of OSS, either private or governmental, which cooperate in providing cover for an operative, are made through the intermediary of a representative of the Director, OSS, appointed for the purpose.

g. In working out the details of an operative's cover, the desk head will have the assistance of the Document Intelligence Division of the Censorship and Documents (CD) Branch. From this Division, the desk head will be able to obtain for his operative the necessary samples of foreign papers, stamps, labels, letterheads, and documents; required items of foreign clothing, accessories, suitcases, dispatch cases, and similar

War correspondents and OSS personnel leave for foreign theaters from the railhead at Camp Patrick Henry, July 9, 1944. (NARA)

equipment; and information on conditions and regulations in foreign countries with which the operative must be familiar.

h. In the event of capture by the enemy, a secret intelligence operative or agent should stick by his cover story and deny all charges. Despite the seriousness of his own position, he should not fail to protect to the end the security of the organization of which he is a member.

17. *COMMUNICATIONS*

a. Good communications are essential to the efficient functioning of an intelligence network. An operative may be able to obtain vital information, but unless he can get that information to the right people in sufficient time, his work will have been wasted. Much thought and effort, therefore, must go into the establishment of a safe, rapid communications system.

b. Communications can be divided into three categories: within a network; between operatives or agents and the field base; and from a field base to other field bases and Washington.

c. Within a network a number of varying methods may be used to maintain communications. These include personal meetings, cutouts, secret inks, improvised codes, and letter drops, and at times telephone, telegraph, ordinary mail, or general delivery. Each of these measures has particular advantages and disadvantages, and each requires special precautions. The method or combination of methods used will be governed by local conditions. If possible, an alternate communications system should be set up and held in readiness to be used if the first system should break down.

d. For communications between a network and a field base, radio is one of the best means in view of its rapidity. When used, adequate security must be taken to avoid enemy detection. Security methods include: keeping the transmission short; changing the transmission time constantly; moving the location of the set frequently; employing cipher. In addition to radio, couriers are a primary means of communication. Sometimes, however, communication can be effected through transport workers, public conveyances, or even more ordinary methods of telephone, telegraph, or mail.

e. In communicating between a field base and other field bases or Washington, existing Army and Navy, State Department, and commercial facilities will be used.

18. ARRIVAL AND DEPARTURE

a. It is essential that careful planning precede an operative's penetration of a new territory and that he be furnished with detailed instructions as to the means of entry and of contacting individuals who will be of assistance to him. This is particularly true of an operative inaugurating SI activities in an enemy or enemy-controlled country.

b. An operative can enter and leave his assigned area of operations either secretly or by the normal means of access and egress under the protection of his cover. An operative may gain secret entry to a territory by airplane, submarine or other vessel, or by making his way across a land border. Particular care must be taken to hide or destroy the paraphernalia an operative may have used to enter a country surreptitiously, such as a parachute or a rubber boat.

c. On arrival in a new area, the operative should learn all he can as quickly but discreetly as possible about local conditions and regulations and local personalities, and should at once plan and make arrangements for his escape in case of emergency.

d. Before he enters a new area, every effort is made to furnish the operative with authentic and current documents, such as identity and ration cards. However, since the enemy authorities may from time to time make changes in the cards currently in effect as a control measure, the operative working in hostile territory should as soon as possible make sure that his documents conform to existing regulations.

e. His first pre-occupation should be to establish himself in his cover and become an accepted member of the community. He should not attempt any undercover work until this preliminary adjustment has been accomplished. The time required to establish himself will depend on where the operative is located, the nature of his cover, his own resourcefulness and the amount of assistance he will receive from friends. Generally speaking, the operative will be able to begin functioning a good deal sooner in a neutral country than in enemy or enemy-occupied territory, where greater precautions must be taken. The operative or agent who is a citizen or resident of the area in which he is to operate has a distinct advantage and will be able to begin his undercover work much sooner.

19. *ESTABLISHING SOURCES OF INFORMATION*

a. In neutral countries, local American business men or those of a friendly nationality can be useful to the operative in making contacts and securing sources of information. Members of the neutral country's secret police and minor government officials, if favorably disposed or sufficiently rewarded, can also be of great assistance. Undercover activities in a neutral country are usually in violation of the laws of the country. Hence, in every case proper security measures must be taken, as well as every precaution against enemy agents in the same area.

b. In enemy and enemy-occupied countries, the operative may receive support and assistance from members of underground organizations and opposition political parties with whom he has established contacts.

c. In the selection of agents, those shall be sought who have direct access to the information desired; first hand information will be more accurate and helpful than hearsay.

d. The number and type of agents an SI operative should recruit will vary with existing local conditions. In general, a secret intelligence network should be kept as small and compact as the mission to be accomplished will allow.

e. In conformity with the basic rule of security that no one in the organization be told more than he needs to know to do his own job, a secret intelligence network may be set up along the lines of the cell system, modified to fit prevailing circumstances. The following diagram represents a type of the cell principle:

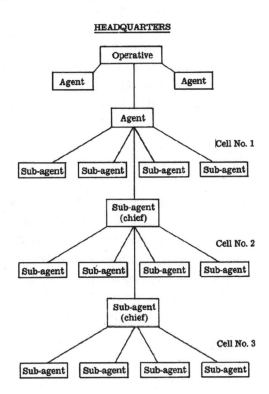

A key man, the operative, would be sent by headquarters to organize a network in a given area. This man would recruit locally one or more agents, none of whom—in case there were more than one—would know the others. The operative alone would communicate directly with headquarters, each of his agents reporting to him. Each agent would then organize a cell, or group, of perhaps four to six sub-agents. These sub-agents would not know the operative, but each would report to the agent in charge of his particular cell. One of the sub-agents from cell number one, selected for his leadership and ability, would then be designated to form and become chief of a second cell. None of the men in cell number two would know the men in cell number one except the chief, who would report to the head of the first cell. One man from cell number two would then be designated to form a third cell, and so on until the desired number of cells was organized. That number would vary with the job to be done and the local situation. As used by SI, this form of cell organization is not rigid, but may be altered to meet special conditions.

f. Before employing a new agent, the operative should conduct a thorough yet unobtrusive security check to make sure of his reliability. The importance of knowing one's man is obvious. Operatives should be particularly wary of individuals who offer their services unsolicited; these may be agents provocateur and operating for the enemy police. After checking a prospective agent for security, the operative should assign him relatively simple tasks at first, gradually building up to more difficult tasks of greater trust.

g. In addition to collecting information· through regularly employed agents, the operative even in enemy or enemy-occupied countries will be able to gather a good deal of general information from the press and radio and through his normal social and business contacts. The individuals furnishing this information, of course, will not be aware of the operative's secret activities. When pieced together in the light of reports received from agents, information gleaned in this manner can prove of value.

[. . .]

A unit of U.S. combat troops, trained by the OSS for guerrilla and insurgency warfare, seen in their quarters before heading overseas. (U.S. Army Signal Corps)

SECTION VI—TYPES OF INFORMATION REQUIRED

31. *GENERAL*

Since the SI Branch has the dual function of servicing OSS and disseminating intelligence to a number of widely different organizations, the type of information it is required to collect is extremely varied. The order of priority for the different types of information will depend on the area in question and the prevailing situation, as well as on the needs of the different organizations for the particular area. The following lists, paragraphs 32–36 inclusive, typical secret intelligence objectives.

32. *MILITARY INFORMATION*

a. ORDER OF BATTLE
Identification, location, strength and movement of enemy troop units, aircraft, materiel, and base supply depots.

b. DEFENSIVE POSITIONS
Gun emplacements (number, type, size, range, and condition of guns). AA defenses; fortifications, block-houses, pill boxes, trenches, and barbed wire entanglements; AT defenses; tank traps, road blocks, land mines; communication and transportation facilities.

c. LANDING BEACHES AND BEACH DEFENSES
Location; length, width, slope and composition; depth of water off shore, shoals, reefs; currents, tide and surf conditions; terrains behind beaches; roads leading from beaches to interior.

d. AIRFIELDS
Location; adjacent topography including landmarks; dimensions; length and position of runways; surface; size of plane capable of using; obstructions near field; hangars; dispersal areas; repair facilities; fuel and oil supplies; communication and transportation facilities; connecting roads and railroads; defenses; camouflage; weather conditions.

e. COMMUNICATIONS
Railroads, roads, waterways, harbors, radio nets, telephone and telegraph systems used by the military. [. . .]

f. RADAR EQUIPMENT
Type; location; how defended; how camouflaged.

g. SECRET WEAPONS AND LATEST TECHNICAL DEVELOPMENTS.

33. *NAVAL INFORMATION*

a. NAVAL SEA AND AIR FORCES

Location; numbers and identification of vessels by types and names; new or unusual types of vessels; secret weapons and devices; movements of vessels; photographs and silhouettes of vessels and aircraft.

b. NAVAL BASES

Location; number and types of vessels present; facilities for construction and repair of vessels, including dry docks; fuel storage and facilities; supply depots; ammunition depots; personnel depots; berthing piers; anchorage ground; air bases; radio stations; radar installations; defenses, land and air, submarine nets and mines.

34. *ECONOMIC INFORMATION*

a. ESSENTIAL WAR INDUSTRIES

Location of plants; type, quantity and quality of production; defenses; camouflage; movement of plants to new locations; effects of bombing; blueprints and plans; sources of supply; labor relations.

b. ELECTRICAL POWER INSTALLATIONS

Location, capacity and defenses of power stations, power dams and high tension lines.

c. TELEPHONE AND TELEGRAPH SYSTEMS

Communication net; location of exchanges; number of wires or cables above or below ground; type and condition of equipment; telephone directories; measures of defense.

d. RADIO COMMUNICATIONS

Location, power, range, wave length and call letters of stations; number, type and condition of receiving sets; best times for reception; measures of defense.

e. RAILROADS

> Location; motive power, steam or electric; if the latter, location of controls, transformers, and substations; signal system; number of tracks; gauge; condition of road-bed, rolling stock and equipment; location of tunnels, bridges, culverts, whether prepared for destruction; repair shops, stations, marshalling yards, sidings, switches and turntables; goods and personnel transported; time tables; measures of defense.

f. ROADS

> Location; width and surface; viaducts, bridges and culverts, with load capacity; road-building equipment; defenses; trucks; buses and cars available; filling stations, gasoline and oil stocks; amount and kind of traffic.

g. WATERWAYS

> Location; width, depth; locks; bridges; barges; defenses; amount and kind of traffic.

h. HARBORS

> Number and size of port facilities; transportation and communication facilities; cranes; storage, refrigeration facilities; fuel facilities; fresh water supplies; labor conditions; measures for defense; number and types of vessels, with destination where possible.

i. In general, all important economic changes, such as: marked shortages; greatly increased production; new factories, transportation and communication facilities; destruction by bombing; repairs to installations damaged by bombing; new defense measures. In addition, SI agents may be called upon for specific information on designated areas, such as water supply and health conditions.

35. POLITICAL INFORMATION

a. PROPOSED CHANGES IN GOVERNMENT POLICY

b. POLITICAL PARTIES
Aims, strength, importance.

c. POLITICAL PERSONALITIES
Venalities, weaknesses, comprising activities; strong and weak
points in ability and character.

d. UNDERGROUND MOVEMENTS
Organization; strength; aims; operations; finances; leaders.

e. LABOR ORGANIZATION
Strength; leaders; policies.

f. POLICE SYSTEM
Organization; methods; important officials.

g. HOSTILE INTELLIGENCE AND COUNTER-INTELLIGENCE SERVICES
Organization; aims; methods; relation to similar organizations
in other countries; effectiveness; descriptions and personal
histories of officials and agents.
(The collection of such information is primarily the responsibility of X-2. However, any information of this nature collected
by SI will be passed on to X-2.)

h. METHODS OF CONTROLLING CIVILIAN POPULATION
Identity cards; curfews; travel permits; rationing and other
regulations; plans for civilian control on D-day. Copies of
identity cards and similar documents should be procured,
together with intelligence for their proper use, to be utilized
by future agents.

i. Where applicable, relations between enemy occupation authorities and civil population; between enemy occupation authorities
and local government; between enemy occupation authorities and
local police.

36. PSYCHOLOGICAL INFORMATION

a. MORALE OF CIVILIAN POPULATION
War workers, foreign labor, miners, farmers, civil servants, etc.

b. MORALE OF THE ARMED FORCES
Relations between officers and men, between various services, between allied enemy troops, between troops and conquered peoples, between military and civilians; effect on morale of pay, food, housing, medical care, equipment, leaves, etc.; discipline; military smartness; sale of equipment.

c. MORALE EFFECTS OF BOMBING

d. POPULAR ATTITUDES TOWARD THE GOVERNMENT, THE ARMED FORCES, THE CHURCH, UNITED NATIONS, AXIS COUNTRIES

e. EFFECTS OF UNITED NATIONS' PW [Psychological Warfare] ON MORALE

f. ENEMY PW METHODS AND RESULTS

g. CLEAVAGES BETWEEN GROUPS OF THE CIVIL POPULATION AND BETWEEN IMPORTANT ELEMENTS OF MILITARY AND GOVERNMENTAL PERSONNEL

★★★

The Welrod pistol was a suppressed handgun designed for use by irregular forces and resistance groups. (Askild Antonsen/CC BY 2.0)

OSS memo

The following text is from an OSS memo dated May 26, 1945. It specifically relates the problems encountered by the OSS' Morale Operations (MO) branch, which was dedicated to conducting psychological warfare against the Axis powers. The central thrust of the memo is that the broader U.S. military has a fundamentally limited understanding of the MO branch's relevance or purpose:

26 May 1945

To: Chief, MO
From: Jan F. Libich
SUBJECT: Presentation of MO Material to Military Authorities

1. Experience has shown that when the aid of the military forces is needed for some MO operation it is often very difficult to explain the point verbally. The meaning of psychological warfare and the targets entered often seem strange to military commanders, and they especially hesitate to contribute the necessary assistance if the task in question would risk the lives of some of their men.

2. For example, AFHQ/Caserta refused at first to allow planes of the 15th Air Force to carry our mailbags and papers into Germany. however, after they had been shown samples of faked German letters and other MO items they became very interested. One General calling others into his office remarked "See what these devils have now thought of!" they then offered their wholehearted cooperation and the necessary orders were obtained within two hours. From then on everyone was enthusiastic, and even the loss of two planes and several fliers of these special missions did not hamper the zeal of those concerned.

3. It is therefore suggested that a standard explanation of MO as a potential weapon of war be printed and submitted to the military authorities concerned, together with samples of MO material each time a new project is contemplated and the services of the military forces are needed.

The Counter Intelligence Corps (CIC) was one of the more controversial U.S. military intelligence-gathering organizations of the war. It was a sizable force, some 5,000 strong by 1945, and its primary duty was to investigate and detect evidence of sedition, subversion, espionage, or sabotage directed against the Army. Naturally, a significant portion of its focus was on potential infiltration by enemy agents, but they also provided more general intelligence through activities such as prisoner interrogation and document analysis. The CIC deployed detachments in the field at the division, corps, army, and theater levels, its NCO-rank operatives notable for wearing either plain clothes or uniforms without insignia.

More controversially, the CIC also investigated its own, monitoring military personnel through a network of informers, whose information eventually led to an output of 150,000 reports every month. The main focus of this covert observation was to identify and keep track of communist sympathizers, but ultimately this work became politically controversial and was curtailed. The following manual explains the power and scope of some of the operational techniques in use in 1943.

★★★

From TM 30-215, *War Department Technical Manual, Counter Intelligence Corps* (1943)

SECTION I
GENERAL

1. Purpose.—a. In addition to the counterintelligence responsibilities recognized in 30-25 and the usual field security counterintelligence mission, there exist other counterintelligence responsibilities which fall upon commanders of geographical areas and which must be assumed by theater commanders and the commanders of units therein, but for which no personnel provision is made in Tables of Organization. These responsibilities are those connected with prevention or neutralization of the activities of enemy agents within the territory occupied. Included in these responsibilities are the need for the prevention of the entrance of enemy spies into the territory and the prevention of their communication of information obtained to the enemy once they are in such territory, together with the neutralization of their espionage activities. Also included is the need for the prevention of the entrance of enemy saboteurs into the territory and the prevention of their reaching installations vital to the military effort. This counterintelligence mission requires personnel particularly trained and specially qualified. The fulfillment of this phase of the counterintelligence mission demands organization upon a territorial

basis, with provision for personnel to remain in the territory, operating without being moved with tactical organizations. The necessity that a number of men in this work be placed undercover for long periods of time and that many operate over extended periods without in any way disclosing their connection with the Army, emphasizes the need for a Corps free from the limitations and the control of smaller tactical units.

b. The mission of the Counter Intelligence Corps is to furnish appropriate commanders with carefully selected personnel specially trained and equipped to assist commanders in the performance of the duties incident to this type of counterintelligence coverage and the mission of field security. It will not serve to replace or assume responsibility for tactical security or countersubversive installations prescribed for all field force units.

c. In order to accomplish this mission, the Counter Intelligence Corps will utilize commissioned and enlisted personnel [who have] been carefully selected and thoroughly trained. This personnel will be fully investigated as to its loyalty, discretion, and basic qualifications prior to its transfer to the Counter intelligence Corps.

d. This manual furnishes the basic principles of the operation of the Counter Intelligence Corps and it will govern the organization, administration, operation and employment of Counter Intelligence Corps personnel. Where applicable, its provisions apply equally to Counter Intelligence Corps activities in the zone of the interior and in theaters of operations.

2. Freedom of action.—a. It is essential to the effective accomplishment of the Counter Intelligence Corps mission that the personnel of the Corps be encouraged to exercise its initiative at the fullest extent and at that it be permitted to operate with minimum restrictions upon its movements or channels of communication. Counter Intelligence Corps credentials and badges will be honored at all times. The personnel of the Corps is frequently entrusted with extremely hazardous and important missions of

a secret nature requiring expeditious action and, when engaged upon such missions, it must not be delayed by the observance of standard customs and prohibitions. Speed is an essential of counterintelligence, and lateral communication between Counter Intelligence Corps echelons is authorized.

b. In order for Counter Intelligence Corps detachments to perform their missions effectively, expeditiously, and in a secret manner, it is essential that the commanding officer of each detachment has full authority, in appropriate circumstances, to direct the movement of his men within the area of his jurisdiction upon his verbal authorization and without either previous or subsequent written orders. It is further advisable that the commanding officer of the Counter Intelligence Corps detachment attached to a theater of operations be designated an assistant adjutant general for purposes of preparing and issuing classified orders to Counter Intelligence Corps personnel.

3. General supervision.—The Assistant Chief of Staff, G–2, War Department, will prescribe policies governing the administration, operation, and employment of the Counter Intelligence Corps. The Military Intelligence Service, War Department, acting through the office of the Chief, Counter Intelligence Corps, will render general supervision over all Counter Intelligence Corps activities, but the immediate supervision of operational activities of the Counter intelligence Corps will be exercised by the commands in which detachments are serving.

4. Function of command.—The employment of the Counter Intelligence Corps is a basic function of command and is an operational activity. The commander of any organization with which Counter Intelligence Corps personnel is serving, is responsible for the proper and effective organization, administration, and employment of such personnel. In the discharge of this responsibility, these commanders will be governed by the policies established pursuant to the provisions of paragraph 3.

5. Jurisdiction.—The jurisdiction of the Counter Intelligence Corps is limited by the counterintelligence jurisdiction of the command with

which it is serving. The extent of this jurisdiction in the zone of the interior will be limited by the Delimitation Agreement of February 22, 1942, entered into by Military Intelligence Division, Office of Naval Intelligence, and the Federal Bureau of Investigation. In departments, and defense, service, and base commands overseas, jurisdiction is limited by the counterintelligence responsibility of the command. In theaters of operations, jurisdiction is limited by the policies of the commanding general of the theater, and by existing international agreements.

6. Power of arrest.—a. The personnel of the Counter Intelligence Corps on duty in the United States has only that power of arrest which all citizens of the United States possess; that is, the power to arrest any person in the act of committing a felony.

b. Counter Intelligence Corps personnel in theaters of operations will have full power and authority to make arrests in cases within its jurisdiction where it is apparent that the arrest being made is essential to the performance of the counterintelligence mission and that its accomplishment is not in violation of any policy of the commanding general of the theater of operations with respect to such enforcement activities.

7. Publicity.—a. The fact of the existence of the Counter Intelligence Corps will not be considered as classified information. However, every effort will be made to keep identities, locations of personnel, and methods of operation confidential. In the event that contact is unavoidably made with individuals connected with the press, radio, or other news agencies, every effort will be made to prevent publicity.

b. Since Counter Intelligence Corps personnel will, from time to time, be used in undercover capacities, identification cards furnished such personnel will bear no military title. This applies particularly to post exchange and gasoline cards. It is deemed advisable that Counter Intelligence Corps personnel be addressed by all concerned as "Mister" during conversations which might divulge the identity of such personnel and its connection with the Counter Intelligence Corps, in a manner which might be detrimental to the Military Intelligence mission. Normally, such personnel will be addressed as "Mister" when in civilian clothing and by military title when in uniform.

c. Emphasis will be placed upon the protection of the identity of Counter Intelligence Corps personnel both in the interest of the mission and to protect the lives of the personnel. The identity of members of the Corps will be disclosed to the minimum number of civilian or military personnel. All members of the Corps are constantly subject to being placed on undercover or other missions where a knowledge by others of their identity would seriously jeopardize the success of the mission and endanger their lives.

SECTION II
ORGANIZATION

8. General.—a. The Counter Intelligence Corps is composed of such commissioned and enlisted personnel as may be authorized by the Chief of Staff, United States Army. Personnel in service commands, departments, and in oversea defense, service, and base commands, and with Army Ground Forces and Army Air Forces organizations, is attached and is carried chargeable to War Department overhead; it is not chargeable to allotments of personnel authorized for such commands. These commands will carry Counter Intelligence Corps personnel as over and above their existing Tables of Organization. Personnel in theaters of operations will be assigned to such theaters and will not be carried as War Department overhead. These theaters will exercise all normal command and administrative functions with the following exceptions:

(1) Neither officers nor enlisted men will be transferred into the Counter Intelligence Corps, nor relieved therefrom, without the prior approval of the Assistant Chief of Staff, G-2 War Department, except in instances of gross inefficiency or for disciplinary reasons.

(2) Enlisted personnel will not be promoted from the classification of agent to the classification of special agent without prior approval of the Assistant Chief of Staff, G-2, War Department.

(3) Enlisted personnel which is commissioned either through Officer Candidate School, or directly, will not be returned to the Counter Intelligence Corps except with the prior approval of the Assistant Chief of Staff, G-2, War Department.

b. The supervision over the Corps rendered by the Military Intelligence Service will be exercised through the Office of the Chief, Counter Intelligence Corps, which office will be organized and operated under the Chief, Military Intelligence Service, War Department.

9. Disposition.—Counter Intelligence Corps personnel will be utilized directly under the supervision and control of the Assistant Chief of Staff, G-2, War Department, when necessary. Normally, however, detachments will be attached or assigned to headquarters of commands which are charged with counterintelligence responsibilities. It is the responsibility of the Assistant Chief of Staff, G-2, War Department, to furnish personnel as provided for theaters of operations, departments, and oversea defense, service and base commands, Army Ground Forces and Army Air Forces, and service commands in the zone of the interior.

a. Service Commands in the zone of the interior.—The Assistant Chief of Staff, G-2, War Department, will furnish to each of the service commands in the zone of the interior, authorization for detachments of appropriate strength. These detachments will be of sufficient strength to provide the personnel necessary in accomplishing Counter Intelligence Corps missions, and to serve as reservoirs of personnel to be relieved from attachment thereto and assigned or attached to other commands as needed.

b. Departments and oversea defense, service and base commands.— Counter Intelligence Corps detachments will be attached to departments and oversea defense, service and base commands in accordance with Tables of Organization, based upon the needs of such commands, and in consideration of the extent of the counterintelligence responsibility of the command. Bases and other departments or commands which are component parts of defense or other larger commands will not normally be furnished detachments, but necessary personnel will be placed with them on detached service by the higher command to which a detachment has been attached.

Army Ground Forces and Army Air Forces units in the zone of the interior.—Counter Intelligence Corps detachments will normally be attached to units of the Army Ground Forces and the Army Air Forces in the zone of the interior for operational and training purposes in accordance with Tables of Organization established for such units. Such personnel will not normally be attached to Army Ground Forces echelons lower than divisions nor to Army Air Forces echelons lower than air forces or the air force commands.

d. Theaters of Operations.—(1) All Counter Intelligence Corps personnel in a theater of operations will be assigned to the headquarters of that theater. The headquarters of the theater will have assigned to it the detachment provided for by its initial Table of Organization. Thereafter, as Army Ground Forces or Army Air Forces units arrive in the theater of operations with Counter Intelligence Corps detachments, those detachments will, after the arrival of the units, be relieved from such attachment by the commanding general of the theater, and assigned to theater headquarters, the theater Table of Organization being thereby automatically increased. The commanding general of the theater of operations may, thereafter, in his discretion, place Counter Intelligence Corps personnel on detached service with such tactical units within the theater as he considers require such personnel. Upon the departure of tactical units from one theater of operations to another, the commanding general of the theater from which the units are leaving, will attach Counter Intelligence Corps detachments of appropriate strength to such units prior to their departure, the Tables of

Organization being, accordingly, altered. These detachments will move to the new destination of the units and there be assigned to the headquarters of the new theater of operations, again with appropriate changes in Tables of Organization.

(2) Theater commanders, in placing Counter Intelligence Corps detachments on detached service with tactical unit within the theater of operations, or attaching such personnel to units departing therefrom, will constantly maintain, to the fullest extent practicable in view of available personnel, adequate Counter Intelligence Corps personnel assigned to the theater headquarters for Counter Intelligence missions vital to the theater of operations and the geographical area covered by it.

10. Replacement of personnel.—Replacements of lost personnel and necessary increases in detachment strength will be furnished to the various commands by the Assistant Chief of Staff, 3-2, War Department, within authorized Tables of Organization, upon request made to him and according to the availability of personnel.

11. Command.—Each Counter Intelligence Corps detachment will be under the command of the senior Counter Intelligence Corps officer thereof, and the commanding officer of the detachment will be responsible for all matters relating to the detachment to the commanding officer of the command with which it is serving, through the Assistant Chief of Staff, G-2, A-2, or S-2, of that command.

12. Internal organization of detachment.—a. The commanding officer of a Counter Intelligence Corps detachment will establish such internal organization within the detachment and make such distribution of Counter Intelligence Corps personnel, through the area involved, as may be directed by the commanding officer of the command with which it is serving. In making such disposition of personnel and establishing such internal organization, the commander of the area will consider fully the mission of the detachment and will carefully weigh the recommendations of the detachment commander.

b. Since the strength of Counter Intelligence Corps detachments furnished to various commands will vary, the internal organization of such detachments will not be uniform. However, in every instance where circumstances permit, the Counter Intelligence Corps headquarters should be established physically removed from the other sections of the command headquarters. When the size of the detachment will permit, it may be organized internally into five sections as follows:

(1) Administrative section.—Personnel required for maintaining records and performing clerical duties.

(2) Counterespionage section.—Personnel whose experience, training, and natural aptitude fit the for counterespionage activity.

(3) Countersabotage section.—Personnel familiar with plant, communication, port, and transportation security, mechanical and electrical engineering, and other allied subjects qualifying them to perform security surveys and make recommendations based thereon.

(4) Technical section.—Personnel with technical training and experience qualifying them to perform duties connected with photography, sound recording, telephone supervision, detection of secret inks, and other technical Investigative activities.

(5) General assignment section.—Personnel not possessing specialized training or experience qualifying them for assignment to one of the above enumerated section.

[. . .]

SECTION VII
OPERATIONS

36. General.—The Assistant Chief of Staff, G-2, War Department, is responsible for the formulation of policies governing the operation of

Counter Corps personnel. The actual operational activities of Counter Intelligence Corps detachments are a function of command and the commanding officer of such a detachment is responsible to the commanding general of the command with which the detachment is serving for the operation of the detachment. He is the operational Counter Intelligence Corps advisor to the G-2, A-2, S-2, or Director of Intelligence of the command concerned. Within the policies established by the Assistant Chief of Staff, G-2, War Department, the control and direction of the operations of Counter Intelligence Corps detachments lies with the commanding officer of the command to which the detachment is attached or assigned and regardless of whether it is assigned or attached. The recommendation of the Counter Intelligence Corps detachment commander should be considered in determining upon missions which may involve Counter Intelligence Corps personnel. In formulating plans for offensive intelligence action, it is advisable that the Counter Intelligence Corps detachment commander be consulted concerning probable enemy counterintelligence measures.

37. Channels of communication.—Counter Intelligence Corps channels of communication are the same as those prescribed for other intelligence organizations. Direct communication between Counter Intelligence Corps detachments of adjacent units is authorized whenever circumstances justify it. Direct communication between commanding officers of Counter Intelligence Corps detachments and the Office of the Chief, Counter Intelligence Corps is authorized on all administrative matters.

38. Credentials and badges.—a. The Assistant Chief of Staff, G-2, War Department, is responsible for the design and procurement of Counter Intelligence Corps credentials and badges. Commands with which Counter Intelligence Corps personnel are serving will requisition necessary credentials and badges together with necessary supplies and instructions required for the issuance of such credentials and badges from the Chief, Counter Intelligence Corps to be issued to the personnel entitled to them. The credentials will be authenticated by the Assistant

Chief of Staff, G-2, A-2, or S-2, or the Director of Intelligence of the command to which the detachment for which credentials or badges are being issued is attached or assigned, and proper records with respect to the possession of the credentials and badges will be maintained by his office. The Office of the Chief, Counter Intelligence Corps, will be advised of the issuance of any badge or credential by the command issuing it, and monthly Reports of Change with respect to badges and credentials will be furnished to the Chief, Counter Intelligence Corps, by every command to which such badges and credentials have been furnished.

b. Counter Intelligence Corps credentials and badges should never be taken to the front lines or elsewhere where there is a serious danger of their loss or capture. Counter Intelligence Corps personnel will be constantly reminded that the careless loss of Counter Intelligence Corps credentials or badges is a serious offense. They will, however, also be instructed that the failure to report such a loss is a more serious offense than the loss itself. Periodic inspections at intervals of not more than three months will be made of Counter Intelligence Corps credentials and badges.

39. Duties and functions of Counter Intelligence Corps detachments.—a. The duties and functions of the Counter Intelligence Corps fall, generally, into two categories: the general investigative, rear echelon mission, including safeguarding military information, securing against the activities of enemy agents and rear echelon counterintelligence functions in general; and the field security mission, including counterintelligence measures performed in forward echelons.

(1) General investigative and rear echelon mission.—This part of the Counter Intelligence Corps mission includes the investigation of cases and other appropriate duties within the scope of the counterintelligence jurisdiction of the command to which the personnel concerned is assigned or attached. The scope of the jurisdiction of the Corps will be limited in the zone of the Interior by the Delimitation Agreement of 22 February, 1942. Overseas it will be limited by existing agreements entered into by

the commanding general of the command or area concerned. Included in this category will be the following general duties:

(a) Provisions of TM 30-205.—Assisting in the establishment and functioning of the provisions of TM 30-205 (Confidential) 27 March 1942, and furnishing investigative coverage with respect to material obtained through the operation of the permissions of that manual, the primary duty of the Counter Intelligence Corps will be investigative work which arises from the provisions of the manual. However, this personnel will render assistance and service in connection with the establishment and functioning of the provisions of that manual. Counter Intelligence Corps personnel will not be used to form an integral part of the organization described in TM 30-205.

(b) Safeguarding military information.—The Counter Intelligence Corps will assist in the enforcement of the provisions of AR 380-5 "Safeguarding of Military Information" and will investigate to determine the responsibility for violations of those regulations. It is a part of the mission of the Corps to conduct surveys to determine measures taken to insure compliance with AR 380-5 and other directives concerning the safeguarding of military information, and to make recommendations through the Assistant Chief of Staff, G-2, A-2, or the S-2, to the commanding officer of the unit surveyed with respect to appropriate measures to be taken to obtain proper security and insure compliance with the security measures taken. Members of the Corps will, periodically, deliver lectures on safeguarding military information to troop units.

(c) Frontier control.—The Counter Intelligence Corps will cooperate with the Corps of Military Police and other military and civil authorities in exercising control at frontiers of territory under the jurisdiction of the command to which such personnel is attached or assigned. This action will include recommending the establishment and assisting in the maintenance of controls and control systems over the entrance of persons, good and information into the territory occupied by the command.

(d) General security against activities of enemy agents.—This will include the following:

1. Investigation of actual or apparent instances of or plans for espionage, sabotage, antiallied propaganda, harmful rumors, Fifth Column activities, disaffection, or other subversive activities within or affecting the armed forces.

2. The performance of security surveys to determine the security of communication, transportation lines, storage and supply facilities, headquarters, and other military activities and installations from adverse actions of enemy agents, and the recommendation of security measures to be taken used upon surveys conducted. However, Counter Intelligence Corps personnel will not be used to accomplish the actual protection of such installations or the implementation of the recommendations made. The function of the Corps in this connection is advisory. This does not preclude the use of Counter Intelligence Corps personnel to make periodic checks with respect to the effectiveness of security measures taken.

3. Recommendations with respect to necessary control of the movements of civilian personnel within the area under the jurisdiction of the command with which the detachment is serving, including suggestions with respect to the establishment of pass systems, restricted areas, refugee control and related matters.

4. The maintenance of constant liaison with Signal intelligence Service and the performance of investigations resulting from intercepts indicating the existence of enemy activity.

(e) General investigative duties.—Counter intelligence Corps personnel will be used to perform other necessary investigative missions, falling within the counterintelligence field. Every effort will be made, however, to prevent the diversion of a large percentage of the strength of the

Corps to the performance of routine investigative duties to the detriment of the performance of the more important counterintelligence missions falling within the jurisdiction of the Corps both in the zone of the interior and overseas.

(2) Field security mission.—The field security mission of the Counter Intelligence Corps will be performed with forward echelons during tactical operations and will be oriented to neutralize the efforts of enemy agents relating to the tactical operation. It will include the securing of information of counterintelligence value with respect to the identity and activities of enemy agents. The performance of these may be continued as follows:

(a) Search of enemy headquarters, billets, and personnel and seizure of significant documents.

(b) Arrest of known enemy agents end dangerous sympathizers.

(c) Establishment of an informer net based upon immediate contact with own friends.

(d) Seizure of telephone exchanges and/or radio stations, arrangements for their protection until they are taken over by proper personnel.

(e) Stopping of all civilian communications by mail, radio, telephone, telegraph and the seizure of all mail and civilian post boxes and of the records of all radio and telegraph stations.

(f) Establishment of contacts with local officials.

(g) In the event of withdrawal, the search of evacuated headquarters, bivouac areas, billets and other installation and areas for documents or material which would be value to the enemy and the safeguarding or destruction, as required by circumstances, of material found.

(h) The control of refugees to prevent enemy infiltration.

b. While division has been made above between the general investigative mission and the field security mission, both come within the general mission of the Counter Intelligence Corps and duties coming within the scope of either will be performed by Counter Intelligence Corps personnel when appropriate whether such personnel be in the zone of the interior, in a theater of operations, in an oversea defense, service or base command, or with a tactical unit of the Army Ground Forces or Army Service Forces either in the zone of the interior or overseas.

c. Counter Intelligence Corps personnel attached to tactical units may be used for routine housekeeping duties when such use will not interfere with the proper performance of its primary functions as outlined in this manual.

40. Coordination.—a. Successful operations of the Counter Intelligence Corps frequently depend upon the rapid and concerted action of several Counter Intelligence Corps detachments or elements thereof. Such teamwork can only be properly developed by close and constant liaison between the commanding officers of Counter Intelligence Corps detachments and individual contacts, where feasible, between the enlisted personnel of such detachments.

b. To accomplish this coordination, the commanding officer of the Counter Intelligence Corps detachment in each theater of operations will maintain close contact with the officers in charge of the detachments throughout his theater and will require these officers to maintain close liaison among themselves at all times. Similarly, in the zone of the interior, the commanding officers of the Counter Intelligence Corps detachments attached to tactical units of higher echelons will maintain close contact with the commanding officers of detachments attached to lower echelons, in order that the activities of all may be coordinated.

41. Liaison with other agencies.—The commanding officers of Counter Intelligence Corps detachments and the personnel of such detachments, both in the zone of the interior and in theaters of

operations, will foster close liaison and mutual cooperation between the Counter Intelligence Corps and the Corps of Military Police in the same area. In theaters of operations, every effort will be made by all Counter Intelligence Corps personnel to establish and maintain cooperation with local law enforcement agencies and the Intelligence and Military Police Organizations of Allied Armies. Emphasis will be placed upon this element of the operations of the Counter Intelligence Corps in theaters of operations.

42. Civil situation overseas.—a. Counter Intelligence Corps detachments entering new areas with tactical units or as the initial detachment assigned to a new theater headquarters will take appropriate steps to become oriented at the earliest practicable moment. The personnel will seek to familiarize itself with local political and economic conditions, racial and religious elements and problems, the particular outstanding customs and characteristics of the civilian population, and the attitude of the population toward the war.

b. Having begun the orientation outlined in a above, the Counter Intelligence Corps detachment will prepare itself, within the policies established by the commanding general of the theater of operations, to make discreet contact with friendly elements in the area and to identify hostile and neutral individuals and groups, taking appropriate action with respect to them. These friendly elements will form the nucleus of informant nets to be established.

43. Special missions.—Counter Intelligence Corps personnel is frequently required to perform special missions involving complicated activities and highly specialized capabilities. The number of individuals selected for a mission of this character will depend upon the mission and the circumstances but, normally, not less than two individuals will be assigned. Whenever practicable, a commissioned officer will be placed in charge of such a mission. It is important that individuals selected for special missions be familiar with each other's methods of operation and have full confidence in each other's ability.

Sources

Chapter 1

U.S. War Department, FM 30-5, *Basic Field Manual, Military Intelligence: Combat Intelligence* (Washington, D.C., Government Printing Office, 1940)

Presidential directions and instructions to the FBI (December 1940 and February 1942)

Chapter 2

U.S. War Department, FM 30-10, *Basic Field Manual, Military Intelligence: Observation* (Washington, D.C., Government Printing Office, 1940)

U.S. Military Intelligence Service, "The Individual Soldier," *Intelligence Bulletin* (Washington, D.C., November 1942)

U.S. War Department, FM 30-15, *Basic Field Manual, Military Intelligence: Examination of Enemy Personnel, Repatriates, Documents and Matériel* (Washington, D.C., Government Printing Office, 1939)

Chapter 3

U.S. War Department, FM 11-35, *Signal Corps Field Manual: Signal Corps Intelligence* (Washington, D.C., Government Printing Office, 1942)

U.S. War Department, FM 11-20, *Signal Corps Field Manual: Organization and Operations in Corps, Army Theater of Operations, and GHQ* (Washington, D.C., Government Printing Office, 1940)

U.S. Military Intelligence Service, "The Individual Soldier," *Intelligence Bulletin* (Washington, D.C., November 1942)

Chapter 4

U.S. War Department, FM 1-40, *Air Corps Field Manual: Intelligence Procedure in Aviation Units* (Washington, D.C., Government Printing Office, 1940)

U.S. War Department, FM 30-21, *War Department Field Manual: Aerial Photography Military Applications* (Washington, D.C., Government Printing Office, 1944)

U.S. War Department, TM 5-246, *War Department Technical Manual: Interpretation of Aerial Photographs* (Washington, D.C., Government Printing Office, 1942)

United States Strategic Bombing Survey, *United States Strategic Bombing Survey Summary Report (Pacific War)* (Washington, D.C., Government Printing Office, 1946)

U.S. War Department, FM 30-20, *Basic Field Manual, Military Intelligence: Military Maps* (Washington, D.C., Government Printing Office, 1940)

Division of Naval Intelligence, ONI 223, *Ship Shapes: Anatomy and Types of Naval Vessels* (Washington, D.C., Navy Department, 1942)

Chapter 5

Office of Strategic Services, Strategic Services Field Manual No.5, *Secret Intelligence Field Manual: Strategic Services (Provisional)* (Washington, D.C., Office of Strategic Services, 1944)

Office of Strategic Services, Memo (May 26, 1945): CIA-RDP13X00001R000100410007-2

U.S. War Department, TM 30-215, *War Department Technical Manual: Counter Intelligence Corps* (1943)